THE NASSAU COUNTY
INTERSCHOLASTIC MATHEMATICS
LEAGUE

BEST MATHLETE
LISA   SHANE
IN

South Side

HIGH SCHOOL
10th Place Individual

19 84 - 19 85

MATHEMATICAL GEMS II

By
ROSS HONSBERGER

THE
DOLCIANI MATHEMATICAL EXPOSITIONS

Published by
THE MATHEMATICAL ASSOCIATION OF AMERICA

———

Committee on Publications
EDWIN F. BECKENBACH, Chairman

The Dolciani Mathematical Expositions

NUMBER TWO

MATHEMATICAL GEMS II

By
ROSS HONSBERGER
University of Waterloo

Published and Distributed by
THE MATHEMATICAL ASSOCIATION OF AMERICA

© 1976 by

The Mathematical Association of America (Incorporated)

Library of Congress Catalog Card Number 76-15927

Complete Set   ISBN 0-88385-300-0

Vol. 2   ISBN 0-88385-302-7

Printed in the United States of America

Current printing (last digit):

10 9 8 7 6 5 4 3 2

The DOLCIANI MATHEMATICAL EXPOSITIONS series of the Mathematical Association of America was established through a generous gift to the Association from Mary P. Dolciani, Professor of Mathematics at Hunter College of the City University of New York. In making the gift, Professor Dolciani, herself an exceptionally talented and successful expositor of mathematics, had the purpose of furthering the ideal of excellence in mathematical exposition.

The Association, for its part, was delighted to accept the gracious gesture initiating the revolving fund for this series from one who has served the Association with distinction, both as a member of the Committee on Publications and as a member of the Board of Governors. It was with genuine pleasure that the Board chose to name the series in her honor.

The books in the series are selected for their lucid expository style and stimulating mathematical content. Typically, they contain an ample supply of exercises, many with accompanying solutions. They are intended to be sufficiently elementary for the undergraduate and even the mathematically inclined high-school student to understand and enjoy, but also to be interesting and sometimes challenging to the more advanced mathematician.

———

The following DOLCIANI MATHEMATICAL EXPOSITIONS have been published.

PREFACE

This book contains fourteen short, expository essays on elementary topics from number theory, combinatorics, and geometry. Mathematics is full of amazing things and these essays are presented in the hope that you will come to know the excitement of some of its most accessible treasures.

No matter what the level, the reader must possess an appropriate background in order to proceed comfortably. To say that a topic is elementary is not necessarily to imply that it is easy or simple. For much of this book, the reader need have little technical knowledge beyond high school mathematics. It is assumed that he is familiar also with the binomial theorem, mathematical induction, and arithmetic congruences. However, it is not expected that the book will be easy reading for many graduates straight out of high school. Some degree of mathematical maturity is presumed, and upon occasion one is required to do some rather careful thinking. It is hoped that the book will be of special interest to high school mathematics teachers and to prospective teachers.

The essays are independent and they may be read in any order. Exercises and references conclude each topic. The reader is encouraged to consider the exercises carefully, for among them are to be found some splendid problems. Complete solutions to the exercises are included.

I would like to take this opportunity to thank Professors Ralph Boas, Henry Alder, David Roselle, and Paul Erdös for generously undertaking a critical reading of various parts of the manuscript and for suggesting many improvements. I am grateful to Dr. Raoul Hailpern for seeing the work through the Publisher. And especially I want to express my gratitude to Professor E. F. Beckenbach who coordinated the entire project.

ROSS HONSBERGER

University of Waterloo

vii

CONTENTS

CONTENTS

CHAPTER 1

THREE SURPRISES FROM COMBINATORICS AND NUMBER THEORY

    In our first story we consider three curious results from the area overlapped by combinatorics and number theory.

    As an easy preliminary to the first one, let us derive the formula for the exponent h of the greatest power of a prime number p which divides $n!$, n a natural number. For example, what is the greatest power of 2 that divides 19!?

$n! = 19! = 1 \cdot 2 \cdot 3 \cdot 4 \cdot 5 \cdot 6 \cdot 7 \cdot 8 \cdot 9 \cdot 10 \cdot 11 \cdot 12 \cdot 13 \cdot 14 \cdot 15 \cdot 16 \cdot 17 \cdot 18 \cdot 19$

Group 1:	×	×	×	×	×	×	×	×	×
Group 2:		×		×		×		×	
Group 3:				×				×	
Group 4:								×	

We can count the number of factors 2 in the product 19! in four groups as follows. Every second number provides a factor of 2 (2, 4, 6, 8, 10, 12, 14, 16, 18); every fourth number possesses a second factor 2 (4, 8, 12, 16); every eighth number has a third 2 (8, 16); and every sixteenth number has a fourth 2 (16). Altogether there are $9 + 4 + 2 + 1 = 16$ factors 2, and $h = 16$. To determine the number of integers in the first group, we divide 19 by 2 and disregard the remainder. This is denoted [19/2], and is called the "integer part" of 19/2. Its value is $[19/2] = [9\frac{1}{2}] = 9$. Similarly, the number of integers contributing a second factor 2 is $[19/2^2] = [4\frac{3}{4}] = 4$, accounting for group 2 (4, 8, 12, 16). The third and fourth groups have, respectively, $[19/2^3] = 2$ and $[19/2^4] = 1$ members. Thus

$$
\begin{aligned}
h &= [19/2] + [19/2^2] + [19/2^3] + [19/2^4] \\
&= \ \ 9 \ \ + \ \ 4 \ \ + \ \ 2 \ \ + \ \ 1 \ \ = 16.
\end{aligned}
$$

In general, we see, in precisely the same way, that

$$h = [n/p] + [n/p^2] + [n/p^3] + \cdots,$$

where the series continues until the powers of p exceed n. When this happens we have $[n/p^i] = 0$ for all succeeding terms and the series terminates.

1. Now, let n denote a natural number, and let g denote the number of 1's in its representation in the binary scale. As above, let h denote the index of the greatest power of 2 which divides $n!$. For example, $n = 47$ has the representation 101111 in the scale of 2, giving $g = 5$. For h we have

$$
\begin{aligned}
h &= [47/2] + [47/2^2] + [47/2^3] + [47/2^4] + [47/2^5] \\
&= \ \ 23 \ \ + \ \ 11 \ \ + \ \ 5 \ \ + \ \ 2 \ \ + \ \ 1 \\
&= \ \ 42.
\end{aligned}
$$

Then, as you have probably guessed already, we always have

$$g + h = n.$$

This result is due to the great French mathematician Adrien Legendre (1752–1833). It is one of the two results we will prove after they have all been stated.

2. Secondly, let n denote a natural number and, again, let g denote the number of 1's in its binary representation. Next, consider the binomial coefficients $\binom{n}{r}$, which arise in the expansion

$$(1 + x)^n = \binom{n}{0} + \binom{n}{1}x + \binom{n}{2}x^2 + \cdots + \binom{n}{n}x^n.$$

As is well known, these coefficients constitute the nth row of the Pascal triangle. Thus we can easily investigate these numbers for small values of n. For all n, however, the number of coefficients $\binom{n}{r}$ (that is, coefficients in row n) which are *odd* numbers turns out to be a power of 2. In fact, for all n, the number of odd $\binom{n}{r}$ is 2^g, a most unexpected result.

n	Pascal Triangle									n in binary	g
0	1									0	0
1	1	1								1	1
2	1	2	1							10	1
3	1	3	3	1						11	2
4	1	4	6	4	1					100	1
5	1	5	10	10	5	1				101	2
6	1	6	15	20	15	6	1			110	2
7	1	7	21	35	35	21	7	1		111	3
8	1	8	28	56	70	56	28	8	1	1000	1
.	.	.	.	.	.	.	.	.		. . .	.

3. The third item is the construction of a sieve for the prime numbers by a simple manipulation of the Pascal Triangle. Instead of writing the numbers in columns with each row beginning at the left, we shift the $n + 1$ entries of row n to occupy places in the columns $2n$ to $3n$, inclusive. Also, the entries in row n which are divisible by n are circled. Then the natural number k is a prime number if and only if all the numbers in column k are circled! [1] (See Figure 1.)

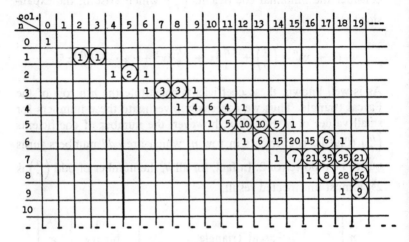

Fig. 1

Proof of Item **1.** Let the binary representation of n be $n = a_k a_{k-1} \cdots a_1 a_0$. Each digit a_i is either 0 or 1, and the number of 1's is g. In expanded form, we have $n = a_0 + a_1 2 + a_2 2^2 + \cdots + a_k 2^k$. Then

$$\left[\frac{n}{2} \right] = \left[\frac{a_0}{2} + a_1 + a_2 2 + \cdots + a_k 2^{k-1} \right]$$

$$= a_1 + a_2 2 + \cdots + a_k 2^{k-1}.$$

In general, for $0 < r \leqslant k$, we have

$$\left[\frac{n}{2^r} \right] = \left[\frac{a_0 + a_1 2 + \cdots + a_{r-1} 2^{r-1}}{2^r} + a_r + a_{r+1} 2 + \cdots + a_k 2^{k-r} \right].$$

Now

$$a_0 + a_1 2 + \cdots + a_{r-1} 2^{r-1} \leqslant 1 + 2 + 2^2 + \cdots + 2^{r-1}$$
$$= 2^r - 1 < 2^r.$$

Thus

$$\frac{a_0 + a_1 2 + \cdots + a_{r-1} 2^{r-1}}{2^r} < 1,$$

whence

$$\left[\frac{n}{2^r} \right] = a_r + a_{r+1} 2 + \cdots + a_k 2^{k-r}.$$

For $r = 1, 2, \ldots, k$, this gives

$$\left[\frac{n}{2} \right] = a_1 + a_2 2 + a_3 2^2 + \cdots + a_k 2^{k-1}$$

$$\left[\frac{n}{2^2} \right] = a_2 + a_3 2 + \cdots + a_k 2^{k-2}$$

$$\left[\frac{n}{2^3} \right] = a_3 + \cdots + a_k 2^{k-3}$$

$$\cdots\cdots\cdots\cdots\cdots\cdots\cdots\cdots\cdots\cdots\cdots$$

$$\left[\frac{n}{2^k} \right] = a_k.$$

Adding gives

$$h = a_1 + a_2(1 + 2) + a_3(1 + 2 + 2^2) + \cdots$$

$$+ a_k(1 + 2 + \cdots + 2^{k-1})$$

$$= a_1(2 - 1) + a_2(2^2 - 1) + a_3(2^3 - 1) + \cdots + a_k(2^k - 1)$$

$$= a_0 + a_1 2 + a_2 2^2 + \cdots + a_k 2^k - (a_0 + a_1 + \cdots + a_k)$$

$$= n - (a_0 + a_1 + \cdots + a_k).$$

But the sum of the digits $a_0 + a_1 + \cdots + a_k$ is simply g, whence $h = n - g$, as required.

Proof of Item 3. Item 3 also yields to a straightforward approach. The table given in the statement of the result verifies the claim for $k = 1, 2, 3$ (indeed, all the way up to $k = 19$). For $k = 2m$, an even number greater than 2, we have $m > 1$, and also that the first entry of row m occurs in column k. But this entry is a 1, and it will not be circled because, for $m > 1$, m does not divide 1. Since even numbers exceeding 2 are composite, the hypothesis is seen to hold for k even.

Suppose, then, that k is odd. We shall show that if k is a prime number p, then every entry in column k is circled, and that if k is composite, then at least one number in column k is uncircled. We observe that the rows, n, which put entries in column k are those for which

$$2n \leqslant k \leqslant 3n,$$

i.e.,

$$\frac{k}{3} \leqslant n \leqslant \frac{k}{2}.$$

A look at row n shows that the entry it puts in column k is $\binom{n}{k - 2n}$ (see Figure 2).

(i) If $k = p$, a prime exceeding 3, the entries in column k are $\binom{n}{p - 2n}$, where

$$\frac{p}{3} \leqslant n \leqslant \frac{p}{2}.$$

col. row		$2n$	$2n+1$	$2n+2$		k		$3n$
	— — — —	—	—	—	—	—	—	—
n	— — —	$\binom{n}{0}$	$\binom{n}{1}$	$\binom{n}{2}$	— —	$\binom{n}{k-2n}$	— — —	$\binom{n}{n}$
	— —	—	—	—	—	—	— —	—

FIG. 2

Since p exceeds 3, we have $1 < n < p$, implying that n and p are relatively prime numbers. This means that n and $p - 2n$ are also relatively prime.

Now, for each of the entries $\binom{n}{p - 2n}$ in such a column, we have

$$\binom{n}{p - 2n} = \frac{n!}{(p - 2n)!\,(3n - p)!}$$

$$= \frac{n}{p - 2n} \cdot \frac{(n - 1)!}{(p - 2n - 1)!\,(3n - p)!}$$

$$= \frac{n}{p - 2n}\binom{n - 1}{p - 2n - 1},$$

giving

$$(p - 2n)\binom{n}{p - 2n} = n\binom{n - 1}{p - 2n - 1}.$$

Accordingly, n divides the left side of this equation. But, since n and $p - 2n$ are relatively prime, we conclude that n divides $\binom{n}{p - 2n}$, and the entry is therefore circled.

(ii) Finally, suppose that k is an odd composite number. As such, it is the product of two or more odd primes. Let p denote an odd prime divisor of k and let

$$k = p(2r + 1)$$

(p will divide into k an odd number of times). Since k is composite, we must have $r \geqslant 1$. Consequently, we have $p \leqslant pr$, and

$$2pr < k = 2pr + p \leqslant 3pr.$$

Thus row $n = pr$ contributes to column k, and its entry there is

$$\binom{n}{k - 2n} = \binom{pr}{p}.$$

We shall show that $n = pr$ does not divide this number, implying that column k has an uncircled number. Attempting the division, we have

$$\frac{1}{pr}\binom{pr}{p} = \frac{1}{pr} \cdot \frac{pr(pr-1)(pr-2)\cdots(pr-p+1)}{1\cdot2\cdot3\cdots p}$$

$$= \frac{(pr-1)(pr-2)\cdots[pr-(p-1)]}{1\cdot2\cdot3\cdots p}.$$

No factor $(pr-i)$ in the numerator is divisible by the prime p because $1 \leqslant i \leqslant p-1$. Since the prime p occurs in the denominator, the fraction does not reduce to an integer, showing that n does not divide the entry. The proof is thus complete.

Item **2.** The proof of Item **2** is considerably more complicated and we shall content ourselves with an outline of one approach to the problem [2].

Observe that the number of odd $\binom{n}{r}$ is the number of $\binom{n}{r}$ which are not congruent to 0 (mod 2). The central step is the derivation of a general formula for the number $T(n)$ of $\binom{n}{r}$ which are not congruent to 0 (mod p), p a prime number. If $n = n_k n_{k-1} \cdots n_1 n_0$ in the scale of p, the formula is

$$T(n) = \prod_{i=0}^{k} (n_i + 1);$$

that is, add one to each digit and multiply. In the scale of 2 the digits are 0 or 1. For $p = 2$, then, the factors of $T(n)$ are 1's or 2's. Each 1 in the binary representation of n gives rise to a 2 in $T(n)$, implying

$$T(n) = 2^g.$$

Exercises

1. Prove that if p is a prime number, then $\binom{2p}{p} \equiv 2 \pmod{p}$.

2. Prove that n divides $\binom{n}{r}$ for all $r = 1, 2, \ldots, n - 1$, if and only if n is a prime number.

References

1. H. Mann and D. Shanks, A necessary and sufficient condition for primality, and its source, J. Combinatorial Theory, Series A, 13 (July 1972) 131.

2. N. J. Fine, Binomial coefficients modulo a prime, Amer. Math. Monthly, 54 (1947) 589; see also Amer. Math. Monthly, 65 (1958) 368 (Problem E1288).

CHAPTER 2

FOUR MINOR GEMS FROM GEOMETRY

1. It has long been known that a certain nine points associated with a triangle always lie on a circle. These points are the midpoints of the sides, the feet of the altitudes, and the so-called Euler points, which are the midpoints of the segments joining the orthocenter (where the altitudes meet) to the vertices. (See Figure 3.) This nine-point circle theorem seems to have been in the air in the late 1700's and early 1800's. While history has credited no individual with the discovery of the theorem, the first explicit statement of it was recorded by Poncelet in 1821, and it was independently established by Feuerbach in 1822. Its easy proof is contained in

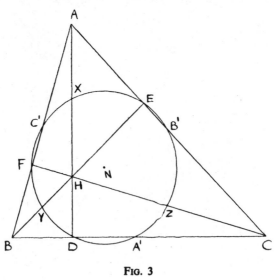

Fɪɢ. 3

10

many books on geometry and at present the theorem is very well known.

But have you ever heard of the **eight-point circle**? This was given in 1944 by Louis Brand of Cincinnati. In 1924, unknown to Brand, C. N. Schmall of New York City wrote of an important special case. However, being even more basic than the illustrious 9-point circle, it is difficult to believe that the giants of the 19th century were not in possession of it.

(i) We prove that a quadrilateral $ABCD$ with perpendicular diagonals has a particular eight points which always lie on a circle. (See Figure 4.) It is well known and easy to establish that the midpoints P, Q, R, S of the sides determine a parallelogram with sides parallel to the diagonals. Since the diagonals are perpendicular, $PQRS$ is a rectangle, and its circumcircle has each of PR and QS as a diameter. Thus this circle also passes through the four feet P', Q', R', S' of the perpendiculars from P, Q, R, S upon the opposite sides.

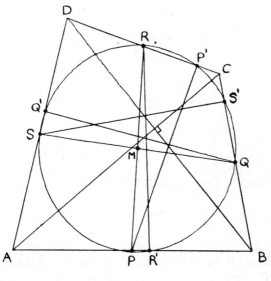

FIG. 4

(ii) Now a triangle with orthocenter H determines a quadrilateral $ABCH$ which has perpendicular diagonals BH and AC. (See Figure 5.) The corresponding eight-point circle contains the midpoints C', A', Z, X and the feet F, D, F, D. (The perpendiculars from midpoints C' and Z meet the opposite sides, CH and AB, respectively, in the same point F. Similarly D occurs twice.) In this instance, then, the eight-point circle reduces to a six-point circle.

From the quadrilateral $BCAH$ we obtain a reduced eight-point circle through the points A', B', X, Y, D, and E. Going through three of the same points as before (A', X, and D), these two eight-point circles must be the same circle. Thus we see that all nine of the points A', B', C', D, E, F, X, Y, Z are concyclic, revealing the nine-point circle to be merely the common eight-point circle of $ABCH$ and $BCAH$ (and also of $CABH$)!

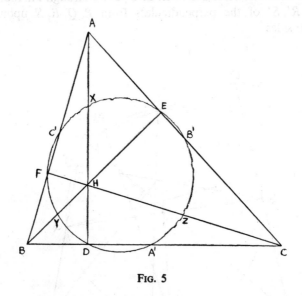

FIG. 5

(iii) Considering again the quadrilateral $ABCD$ in (i), we see that the center M of the eight-point circle is the midpoint of diameter PR. Now suppose a unit mass is suspended from each vertex A, B, C, D. The masses at A and B are equivalent to a mass of two units suspended at their midpoint P. Similarly, the masses at C and D are equivalent to a mass of two units at R. The center of gravity of the whole system, then, is the eight-point center M, the midpoint of PR.

Applying this result to the triangle ABC with orthocenter H in (ii), we see that the nine-point center N, which is really two coincident eight-point centers, is the center of gravity of a system of unit masses suspended at the vertices A, B, C, H of the quadrilaterals involved. (See Figure 6.) However, unit masses at A, B, and C are equivalent to a mass of 3 at the centroid G of triangle ABC. A unit mass at each of A, B, C, H, then, is equivalent to a unit mass at H and 3 units at G. Since N is the center of gravity of the system, it must be that H, N, and G lie in a straight line and, in order to balance the moments about N, HN must equal $3GN$. Thus we have arrived most comfortably at the result that N divides HG internally in the ratio of $3 : 1$.

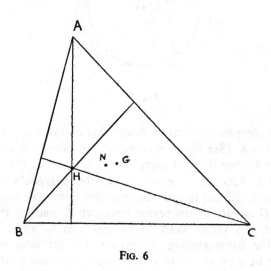

FIG. 6

2. It often happens that a maximum or minimum property of a class of figures is found to reside in the most regular of the figures.

It is a classic result that of all polygons with a fixed number of sides n which circumscribe a given circle K, the regular n-gon has the least area. A most impressive proof of this theorem was given in 1947 by the eminent Hungarian geometer L. Fejes Tóth (pronounced Feh-yesh Tote).

The key move in his thought is the construction of the circumcircle C of the regular n-gon P that circumscribes K. Thus C and K are concentric. In C, the sides of P all cut off the same size minor segment s because each side is the same distance from the common center O. Accordingly, the area of P is $C - ns$. (See Figure 7.)

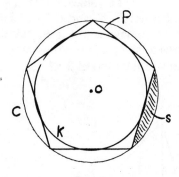

Fig. 7

Now we compare the area of P with that of any n-gon Q which circumscribes K. (See Figure 8.) Since all the sides of P and Q are tangents to K, their distance from the common center O is just the radius r of K. Accordingly, each side of either polygon which goes clear across C will cut from it the same size minor segment s. If a vertex of Q occurs in the region betweeen K and C, the sides meeting at this vertex need to be extended to strike C and complete the corresponding segments s. Let the sides of Q be extended where necessary to yield n equal segments s which we denote, in order around C, by $s_1, s_2, \ldots, s_n$.

Now we work out the area $\overline{Q}$ of the intersection of Q and C. We

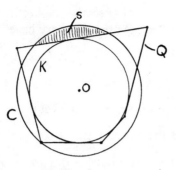

FIG. 8

obtain this area by beginning with the whole circle C and subtracting the areas cut from C by the sides of Q. Except for sides meeting at a vertex between K and C, each side of Q cuts a full segment s from C. For sides which meet between K and C, we have a pair of consecutive segments s_i and s_{i+1} (each of area s) which overlap. (See Figure 9.) Deducting an area s for each of s_i and s_{i+1} would take away their intersection $s_i s_{i+1}$ twice. Thus the area Q is obtained by subtracting from C an area s for each side, provided the intersections $s_i s_{i+1}$ are added back in as compensation. Consequently,

$$\overline{Q} = C - ns + (s_1 s_2 + s_2 s_3 + \cdots + s_n s_1).$$

In the event that s_i and s_{i+1} do not overlap, the intersection $s_i s_{i+1}$ is zero and its inclusion in the expression for $\overline{Q}$ has no effect.

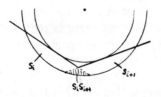

FIG. 9

Since $\overline{Q}$ is that part of Q (perhaps all of it) which lies in C, the area $\overline{Q}$ cannot exceed Q itself. Thus we have

$$Q \geqslant \overline{Q}$$
$$= C - ns + (s_1 s_2 + s_2 s_3 + \cdots + s_n s_1)$$
$$\geqslant C - ns \text{ (since the bracket is not negative)}$$
$$= P, \text{ the regular } n\text{-gon}.$$

Now, if Q has any vertex outside C, part of Q projects beyond C and we have $Q > \overline{Q}$. And if Q has any vertex between K and C, we have $s_1 s_2 + s_2 s_3 + \cdots + s_n s_1 > 0$, giving

$$C - ns + (s_1 s_2 + s_2 s_3 + \cdots + s_n s_1) > C - ns.$$

Thus, unless Q has all its vertices on C, we have $Q > P$. And if Q has all vertices on C, then Q is also a regular n-gon, implying $Q \equiv P$. The conclusion follows.

3. An ingenious new proof of an old chestnut is almost bound to become a hit because our previous association with the problem makes for quick appreciation. It is therefore my hope that you have already come across the following "hardy perennial":

In $\triangle OA_1 A_2$, $\angle O = 20°$ and $OA_1 = OA_2$, $\angle OA_2 X = 20°$ and $\angle OA_1 Y = 30°$. Determine $\theta = \angle A_2 XY$. (See Figure 10.)

The following solution was given in 1951 by S. T. Thompson of Tacoma, Washington. (See Figure 11.)

In the circle C with center O and radius OA_1, $A_1 A_2$ is a chord which subtends a 20° angle at the center. Thus $A_1 A_2$ is the side of a regular 18-gon inscribed in C. Let $A_1 A_2 A_3 \cdots A_{18}$ denote such an 18-gon. Now the amazing thing is that the chord $A_3 A_{15}$ cuts across $\triangle OA_1 A_2$ right through the special points X and Y. In order to justify labelling these intersections X and Y, we will show that the angles $OA_2 X$ and $OA_1 Y$ are indeed 20° and 30°, respectively.

First of all we observe that the chords $A_3 A_{15}$ and $A_1 A_7$ are the same length, each spanning 6 sides of the 18-gon, and are symmetric with respect to the radius OA_2. Thus they cross on OA_2,

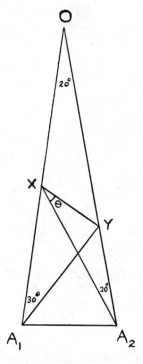

FIG. 10

implying that A_1A_7 passes through Y. Spanning 6 sides of the 18-gon, A_1A_7 extends one-third the way around the circle, and therefore subtends 120° at O. In isosceles triangle OA_1A_7, then, we have $\angle OA_1A_7$, which is $\angle OA_1Y$, equal to 30°.

Joining every third vertex of the 18-gon yields a regular hexagon in C, and the side of an inscribed regular hexagon is just the radius. Thus the chord $A_{15}A_{18}$ is equal to the radius OA_{15}, implying A_{15} is a point on the perpendicular bisector of OA_{18}. Similarly, A_3 is another point on this line, and we conclude that $A_{15}A_3$ is actually the perpendicular bisector of OA_{18}. Since X lies on this perpendicular bisector, we have $OX = XA_{18}$. However, symmetry clearly gives $XA_{18} = XA_2$. Thus $OX = XA_2$, making $\triangle OXA_2$ isosceles and $\angle OA_2X = \angle XOA_2 = 20°$, as claimed.

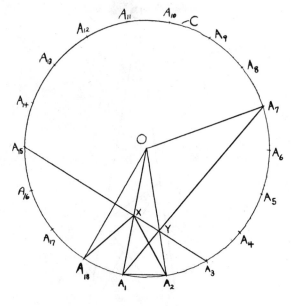

FIG. 11

The rest is easy. The single side A_1A_{18} subtends 20° at O. Since OA_{18} and $A_{15}A_3$ are perpendicular, we have $\angle OXA_{15} = 70°$. The vertically opposite $\angle A_1XY$ is likewise 70°. But exterior angle A_1XA_2 (for $\triangle OXA_2$), being the sum of the two opposite interior angles, is 40°. Thus $\theta = \angle A_2XY = 70° - 40° = 30°$.

4. In the twentieth century one does not hold out much hope that there remain to be discovered really pretty theorems at the most elementary level of geometry. However, the American geometer Roger Johnson seems to have been the first to come across the following result which is well within the reach of any grade 10 or 11 student taking a first course in Euclidean geometry. Johnson encountered the theorem in 1916. We use $C(r)$ to denote the circle with center C and radius r. (See Figure 12.)

THEOREM. *Suppose three equal circles $C_1(r)$, $C_2(r)$, $C_3(r)$ pass through a point O and have second points of intersection P_1, P_2, P_3.*

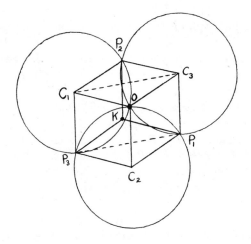

FIG. 12

Then the circumcircle of $\triangle P_1P_2P_3$ is a fourth circle of the same radius r.

Proof. Since the three given circles all have radius r, the figure contains various rhombi. From the two $C_1P_3C_2O$ and $OC_2P_1C_3$, we see that C_1P_3 is equal and parallel to OC_2 which, in turn, is equal and parallel to C_3P_1. Thus C_1P_3 is equal and parallel to C_3P_1, making $C_1P_3P_1C_3$ a parallelogram. Hence opposite sides C_1C_3 and P_1P_3 are equal. Similarly, each of the other two sides of $\triangle C_1C_2C_3$ is equal to a side of $\triangle P_1P_2P_3$, implying the triangles are congruent. But $OC_1 = OC_2 = OC_3 = r$, showing that the circumcircle of $\triangle C_1C_2C_3$ is just $O(r)$. The congruent $\triangle P_1P_2P_3$ has an equal circumcircle, completing the proof.

Frank Bernhart, a colleague at the University of Waterloo, recently pointed out another pleasing completion to this argument. Let K complete rhombus $P_1C_2P_3K$. Then $KP_1 = KP_3 = r$, and since P_2C_3 is equal and parallel to C_1O and P_3C_2, it bears the same relation to P_1K and the figure $P_2C_3P_1K$ is another rhombus. Thus $KP_2 = r$, and the circle $K(r)$ passes through P_1, P_2, and P_3.

It is interesting to note that Frank hit upon this idea by interpreting the figure as the plane projection of a cube, of which O and K represent a pair of opposite vertices.

Also in 1916, Arnold Emch of the University of Illinois gave another delightful proof. (See Figure 13.) Since the given circles are equal, OP_1 cuts off equal segments in the two circles in which it is a chord. Consequently it subtends equal angles x at P_2 and P_3 on the circumferences of these segments. Similarly, common chord OP_2 subtends equal angles y at P_1 and P_3. Now, in $\triangle OP_1P_2$, the sum of the three angles x, y, z is 180°. Thus the angle $P_2P_3P_1$ (which equals $x + y$) is the supplement of $z = \angle P_2OP_1$. However, a cyclic quadrilateral AP_2OP_1 also provides the supplement of z at A. Hence $\angle A = x + y = \angle P_2P_3P_1$. This means that chord P_1P_2 must cut from the circumcircle of $\triangle P_1P_2P_3$ the same size segment that it does from the circle $C_3(r)$. The circumcircle, then, must be the same size as $C_3(r)$.

Among other things, Dr. Emch also drew attention to an application concerning the transformations of the sides of a triangle and its circumcircle under circular inversion in the incircle. Since points on the circle of inversion are invariant, and lines not through the center of inversion are carried into circles through the center of inversion, we see that the sides of the triangle go into

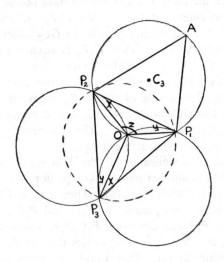

FIG. 13

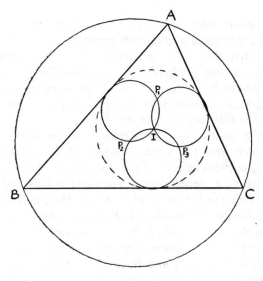

FIG. 14

circles which touch the incircle and pass through the incenter I (points outside the circle of inversion are carried into points inside the circle of inversion). (See Figure 14.) Their diameters are thus the radius of the incircle, implying the three image circles are the same size. By our little theorem, then, the circle through their second points of intersection P_1, P_2, P_3 is again the same size. But this circle is the image of the circumcircle of the triangle. (A vertex, lying on two sides, is transformed to lie on two image circles; also, a circle not through I is taken into another circle not through I.) Thus we have the nice result:

Under inversion in the incircle of a triangle, the sides and the circumcircle are carried into four equal circles.

Exercises

1. X is a point outside angle ABC. Draw a line through X to cut from $\angle ABC$ a triangle of given (suitable) perimeter p.

2. X is a point inside angle ABC. Draw a line through X to cut from $\angle ABC$ a triangle of minimum perimeter.

3. Prove that the points of contact of a skew quadrilateral which circumscribes a sphere are concyclic. (Hint: suspend appropriate masses from the vertices of the quadrilateral so that those at adjacent vertices have as center of gravity the point of contact on the side they determine.)

4. A pirate decided to bury a treasure on an island near the shore of which were two similar boulders A and B and, farther inland, three coconut trees C_1, C_2, C_3. Stationing himself at C_1, the pirate laid off C_1A_1 perpendicular and equal to C_1A and directed outwardly from the perimeter of $\triangle AC_1B$. He similarly laid off C_1B_1 perpendicular and equal to C_1B and also directed outwardly from the perimeter of $\triangle AC_1B$. He then located P_1, the intersection of AB_1 and BA_1. Stationing himself at C_2 and C_3, he similarly located points P_2 and P_3 and finally buried his treasure at the circumcenter of $\triangle P_1P_2P_3$.

Returning to the island some years later, the pirate found that a big storm had obliterated all the coconut trees on the island. How might he find his buried treasure?

5. Given that AB is a diameter of a given circle (center not known), construct using just a straightedge the perpendicular to AB from a given point P.

References

1. L. Brand, The eight-point circle and the nine-point circle, Amer. Math. Monthly, 51 (1944) 84.

2. L. F. Toth, New proof of a minimum property of the regular n-gon, Amer. Math. Monthly, 54 (1947) 589.

3. For Thompson's solution, see Amer. Math. Monthly, 58 (1951) 38, Problem E 913.

4. R. A. Johnson, A circle theorem, Amer. Math. Monthly, 23 (1916) 161.

5. C. N. Schmall, Amer. Math. Monthly, 32 (1925) 99 (Problem 3080, posed in 1924, p. 255).

CHAPTER 3

A PROBLEM IN CHECKER-JUMPING

1. Everybody knows the leap-frog jump in the game of checkers. There is an interesting problem about checker-jumping on the lattice points of a plane. One begins by arranging a number of men in the starting zone, which consists of the half-plane of lattice points on and below the x-axis. The object is to get a man as far as possible above the x-axis by checker-jumps in the directions of the lattice lines (diagonal jumps are not allowed). The problem is to determine the *least* number of men in the starting zone which permits a man to reach a prescribed height above the x-axis.

(i) We see immediately that only two men are needed to reach the first level above the x-axis (i.e., the line $y = 1$). (See Figure 15.)

(ii) It is almost as obvious that level two can be reached with four men. (See Figure 16.)

(iii) In order to reach the third level it is necessary to start with eight men: we use four men to put a man at level two, as just described, and then use another four men to complete the job. (See Figure 17.)

(iv) At this rate one would expect that the number of men required to get to level four would be $2^4 = 16$. Surprisingly, it takes 20. (See Figure 18.) After the 12 moves shown we obtain the configuration of 8 men which was just described for reaching level three. Since this configuration is one unit higher to begin with, it enables a man to reach level four.

2. The main question is the case of level five. The preceding cases have used 2, 4, 8, and 20 men. How many men do you think

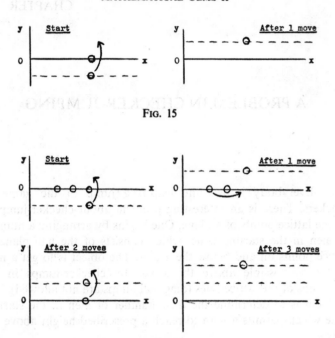

FIG. 15

FIG. 16

it will take to get to level five? Incredibly, the answer is that no arrangement, with however many men, is sufficient to reach level five! The proof is not difficult and one can scarcely remain untouched by the delightful power which mathematics displays in this neat application. This is the discovery of John Conway, of Cambridge.

We begin by noting that if one were able to reach a particular lattice point P on level five, one could, by doing the same thing from a starting position farther to the left or to the right, arrive at any specified lattice point on level five. It's all or nothing for level five. We settle the matter by showing that an arbitrary but definite lattice point P on level five is inaccessible.

We introduce mathematics to the situation by assigning a place-value to every lattice point in the plane. Every value is a power of a number x, a number which shall be specified shortly. The

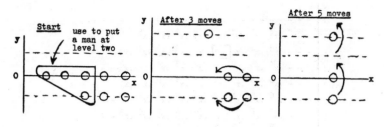

Fig. 17

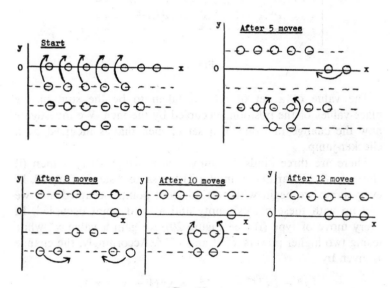

Fig. 18

exponent of the power is simply the number of unit steps in directions parallel to the axes in a shortest path from the distinguished point P to the lattice point in question. Thus P, itself, bears the value x^0, or 1; the four lattice points adjacent to P are valued at x, the eight lattice points which are two steps from P have value x^2, and so on. As a result, the rows and columns of lattice points are assigned sequences of consecutive powers of x. (See Figure 19.)

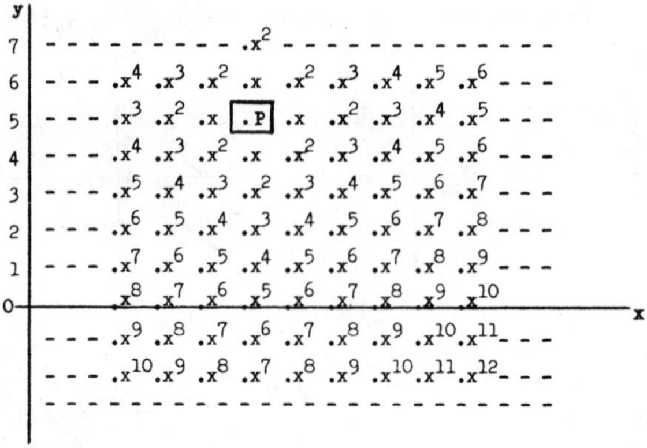

FIG. 19

The value of a set of men is taken to be the sum of the place-values of the positions occupied by the men. We investigate now the change in value of a set of men that is incurred by a checker-jump.

There are three kinds of jumps—those which carry a man (i) closer to P, (ii) farther from P, (iii) the same distance from P. In every jump we begin with two adjacent points occupied and we end up with these places empty and a third point occupied. In every move of type (i) (see Figure 20), we gain a value x^n while losing two higher powers x^{n+1} and x^{n+2}. Accordingly, the change is given by

$$x^n - (x^{n+1} + x^{n+2}) = x^n(1 - x - x^2).$$

For a move of type (ii), we obtain a change in value of $x^{n+2} - (x^{n+1} + x^n) = x^n(x^2 - x - 1)$. Now it is time to specify the number x. We choose x so that there is no change in value for a jump of type (i). For this we need

$$1 - x - x^2 = 0.$$

Thus $x = (-1 \pm \sqrt{5})/2$. Taking x to be the positive root, $(\sqrt{5} - 1)/2$, we obtain a value between 0 and 1. In fact, x is the

A Typical Move of Type (i)

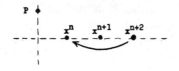

FIG. 20

reciprocal of the famous Golden Mean, which crops up in so many different contexts. Note that $x^2 = 1 - x$. For a move of type (ii), then, we see that the change in value is

$$x^n(x^2 - x - 1) = x^n(1 - x - x - 1) = x^n(-2x) < 0.$$

After a move of type (ii), then, the value of the men remaining is less than the value of the set of men before the move was made. Because a move of type (iii) is merely a jump across one of the two lattice lines which pass through P, we see that a move of type (iii) also reduces the value of a set of men: $x^n - (x^{n-1} + x^n) = -x^{n-1}$. (See Figure 21.) In summary, every jump either leaves the value of a set of men unchanged or it makes it less; under no circumstances does the value increase.

A man at the point P would have, itself, the value 1. Thus a set of men capable of sending a man to the point P would have to begin with a value of at least 1. A set with value less than 1 would require its value to be increased in order to place a man at P, and this cannot be achieved through checker moves. Now the value of the entire half-plane which constitutes the starting zone is easily

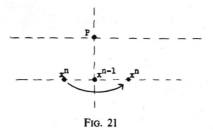

FIG. 21

determined by considering the points in columns. The column directly below P contributes the values $x^5 + x^6 + x^7 + \cdots$, a geometric progression with sum $x^5/(1 - x)$ (recall that $0 < x < 1$). The two columns, one on each side of this "central" one, each gives

$$x^6 + x^7 + x^8 + \cdots = \frac{x^6}{1 - x}, \text{ for a total of } \frac{2x^6}{1 - x}.$$

Similarly there are two columns $x^7 + x^8 + x^9 + \cdots$, for a total of $2x^7/(1 - x)$. Altogether, the grand total for the infinity of columns is

$$S = \frac{x^5}{1 - x} + 2\left(\frac{x^6}{1 - x} + \frac{x^7}{1 - x} + \frac{x^8}{1 - x} + \cdots \right),$$

the latter bracket being a geometric progression. Evaluating the series, and using $1 - x = x^2$, we obtain

$$S = \frac{x^5}{1 - x} + \frac{2x^6}{1 - x}(1 + x + x^2 + \cdots)$$

$$= \frac{x^5}{1 - x} + \frac{2x^6}{1 - x} \cdot \frac{1}{1 - x}$$

$$= x^3 + 2x^2 = x(x^2 + 2x) = x(1 - x + 2x)$$

$$= x(1 + x) = x + x^2 = x + 1 - x = 1.$$

Thus even a single unoccupied place in the starting zone means that the starting set has a value < 1, and this is too small to send a man to level five.

CHAPTER 4

THE GENERATION OF PRIME NUMBERS

1. A formula for the prime numbers has led us a merry chase and always eluded our grasp. However, our efforts have not gone unrewarded, and the topic of this chapter is an exciting advance that has recently been discovered.

In 1772, Euler pointed out that the trinomial

$$f(x) = x^2 + x + 41$$

provides a prime number for each of the forty values $x = 0, 1, \ldots, 39$. Since $f(x - 1) = f(-x)$, we have

$$f(0) = f(-1), \; f(1) = f(-2), \; f(2) = f(-3), \ldots,$$

showing that the trinomial yields these primes again for $x = -1, -2, \ldots, -40$. Thus $x^2 + x + 41$ yields primes for the eighty consecutive integers $x = -40, -39, \ldots, 38, 39$. Equivalently, the function

$$f(x - 40) = x^2 - 79x + 1601$$

gives these eighty prime values for $x = 0, 1, 2, \ldots, 79$. At present this shares the record for the longest string of consecutive integers for which a quadratic yields prime numbers exclusively. (The function $x^2 - 2999x + 2248541$ also yields 80 primes for $x = 1460, 1461, \ldots, 1539$.) Little competition is provided by $6x^2 + 6x + 31$, which is prime for $x = 0, 1, \ldots, 28$. The binomial $2x^2 + 29$ does better, giving 57 consecutive primes for $x = -28, -27, \ldots, 28$. Euler's trinomial is not without other interesting properties, too. (See the exercises.) For example, $f(x)$ is never a square, except for $f(40) = f(-41) = 41^2$, and $f(x)$ is never divisible by any integer between 1 and 41.

Little is known about this general subject, but a few interesting results have been discovered. In 1933, D. H. Lehmer showed that if the particular form $x^2 + x + A$, where $A > 41$, follows the example of $x^2 + x + 41$ and yields primes for all $x = 0, 1, \ldots, A - 2$, then A must be greater than one and a quarter billion. In 1934, it was shown that even in the realm of large numbers there could not be more than one such number A, and in the late 1960's it was shown, after a difficult argument, that there was not even one value. It has been proved that for any n there is an integral polynomial of degree n which takes prime values for $x = 0, 1, 2, \ldots, n$. We note that the function $f(x) = x$ trivially yields all the primes for natural x. However, no polynomial of degree two or more is known to take prime values for any infinity of natural x. It is not difficult to show that no polynomial can yield a prime number for *every* $x = 0, 1, 2, \ldots$.

If we go beyond polynomials we find there are functions which take prime values infinitely often. W. H. Mills proved that there is a real number k such that

$$\left[k^{(3^n)} \right],$$

where $[z]$ denotes the greatest integer not exceeding z, is a prime number for every $n = 1, 2, 3, \ldots$. Mills proved the existence of k but its value is unknown. In 1963, B. M. Bredihin proved that

$$f(x, y) = x^2 + y^2 + 1$$

takes a prime value for infinitely many integral pairs (x, y). However $x^2 + y^2 + 1$ does not even come close to yielding prime values exclusively (e.g., odd^2 + even^2 + 1 = even). Our main interest in this essay is a simple function $f(x, y)$ which, for natural numbers x and y, yields prime numbers *exclusively*, yields *every* prime number, and takes the value of *every odd prime number exactly once*.

2. Wilson's Theorem. Our main result follows easily from one of the pillars of number theory—Wilson's theorem. This theorem was noted by Leibniz almost 300 years ago and it was first proved by Lagrange about 200 years ago. Indeed, Wilson never did prove the theorem; he only guessed it. You may well ask how it came to be known as Wilson's theorem. In 1770, Edward Waring announced the theorem in his writings and he ascribed it to Sir John Wilson because it was Wilson who had told him about it.

In any event, the theorem is a remarkable result. It gives a necessary and sufficient condition for a number to be a prime number, thereby, theoretically at least, providing another way of distinguishing the primes.

WILSON'S THEOREM. *The number p divides $(p-1)! + 1$ if and only if p is a prime.*

Proof. (a) *Necessity.* In this case we are given that p divides $(p-1)! + 1$. Suppose, however, that p is not a prime number. This means that, for some natural numbers a and b, each exceeding 1, we have $p = ab$. The number b, then, is less than p, itself, and therefore occurs as one of the factors in the product $(p-1)!$. Thus b divides $(p-1)!$. But because p divides $(p-1)! + 1$, its own factor b will also divide this number. Dividing both $(p-1)!$ and $(p-1)! + 1$, b must divide their difference, namely 1. However, b exceeds 1, giving a contradiction.

(b) *Sufficiency.* Here we are given that p is a prime and we show that it divides $(p-1)! + 1$. The result is clearly true for $p = 2$. Suppose, then, that p is an odd prime.

Consider the numbers $1, 2, 3, \ldots, p - 1$. We shall show that, if x is one of these numbers, there is also a unique number y among them such that $xy \equiv 1 \pmod{p}$. That is to say, the numbers pair off uniquely so that for each pair we have $xy \equiv 1 \pmod{p}$.

To this end, let x denote such a number, and consider the multiples of x: $[x, 2x, 3x, \ldots, (p-1)x]$. Suppose, if possible, that some two of these are congruent $\pmod{p}$:

$$rx \equiv sx \pmod{p}, \quad \text{where } r \neq s.$$

Then $(r - s)x \equiv 0 \pmod{p}$. This means that p divides $(r - s)x$. Since p is a prime, p must divide either $r - s$ or x (or both). But this is not so, for x, r, and s all belong to the set $(1, 2, 3, \ldots, p - 1)$, making $0 < |r - s|, x < p$. Accordingly, each of these $p - 1$ multiples is congruent to a different remainder $\pmod{p}$. Clearly, none of them is divisible by p. Thus, collectively $[x, 2x, \ldots, (p - 1)x]$ determine all the nonzero remainders $1, 2, \ldots, p - 1$. Consequently, one of them, and only one (xy), yields the remainder 1, as claimed.

Now, among our numbers there are two which pair up with themselves. In order to identify them, consider

$$x^2 \equiv 1 \pmod{p}.$$

This gives $p | x^2 - 1 = (x - 1)(x + 1)$, implying $p | x - 1$ or $p | x + 1$. Clearly the only numbers among $1, 2, \ldots, p - 1$ which satisfy one or the other of these conditions are 1 and $p - 1$. Casting them out leaves the set $(2, 3, \ldots, p - 2)$, where each of the numbers x pairs with a unique different number y to give $xy \equiv 1 \pmod{p}$. Suppose the pairs are denoted

$$x_1 y_1 \equiv x_2 y_2 \equiv \cdots \equiv 1 \pmod{p}.$$

Then the product also satisfies

$$(x_1 y_1)(x_2 y_2) \cdots \equiv 1 \pmod{p}.$$

But the factors on the left side here are just a rearrangement of our set $(2, 3, \ldots, p - 2)$. Thus we have

$$2 \cdot 3 \cdots (p - 2) \equiv 1 \pmod{p},$$

giving $1 \cdot 2 \cdot 3 \cdots (p - 2)(p - 1) \equiv p - 1 \equiv -1 \pmod{p}$, and

$$(p - 1)! + 1 \equiv 0 \pmod{p},$$

as required.

3. The Function $f(x, y)$. Now it is easy to establish that the function

$$f(x, y) = \frac{y - 1}{2} \left[|B^2 - 1| - (B^2 - 1) \right] + 2,$$

where $B = x(y + 1) - (y! + 1)$, x and y natural numbers, generates only prime numbers, every prime number, and each odd prime number exactly once.

Proof. For all natural x and y, the value of B is an integer. Thus B^2 is a nonnegative integer. Accordingly, there are the two cases: (a) $B^2 \geqslant 1$, and (b) $B^2 = 0$.

(a) $B^2 \geqslant 1$: If $B^2 \geqslant 1$, then $B^2 - 1 \geqslant 0$, implying that $|B^2 - 1| = B^2 - 1$. This makes $f(x, y) = 2$, a prime.

(b) $B^2 = 0$: For $B^2 = 0$ the value of the function is

$$f(x, y) = \frac{y - 1}{2} \left[|-1| - (-1) \right] + 2$$

$$= \frac{y - 1}{2} [1 + 1] + 2 = y - 1 + 2 = y + 1.$$

In this case, however, B itself must also be 0, implying that the numbers substituted for x and y make

$$x(y + 1) - (y! + 1) = 0, \quad \text{or} \quad x(y + 1) = y! + 1.$$

Accordingly, the number $y + 1$ divides $y! + 1$. By Wilson's theorem, then, the number $y + 1$ is a prime. Consequently, $f(x, y)$ yields prime numbers exclusively.

We note that $f(1, 1) = 2$. Let p denote an odd prime number. Then, using

$$y = p - 1 \quad \text{and} \quad x = \frac{1}{p} \left[(p - 1)! + 1 \right]$$

(x is guaranteed to be a natural number by Wilson's theorem), we see that $f(x, y)$ yields the prime p: from the definitions of x and y, we have

$$xp = (p - 1)! + 1 \quad \text{and} \quad p = y + 1;$$

then $xp = x(y + 1) = (p - 1)! + 1 = y! + 1$, making $B = 0$ and $f(x, y) = y + 1 = p$. Thus f yields every prime number.

Since f yields only the values 2 and $y + 1$, an odd prime p can arise only as $y + 1$. Thus in every pair (x, y) which makes $f(x, y)$ yield the odd prime p, we must have $y = p - 1$. However, f will yield the odd number $y + 1$, rather than 2, only when $B = 0$. Thus the pair (x, y) must also make $x(y + 1) = y! + 1$. This means that x must have the value $(y! + 1)/(y + 1)$. The single choice for y, then, leads to a single value for x, yielding the unique pair

$$(x, y) \equiv \left(\frac{(p - 1)! + 1}{p}, p - 1 \right)$$

(x is natural by Wilson's theorem),

which makes f take the value p. Thus, while f produces the number 2 "most of the time," it yields each odd prime exactly once.

4. A Remarkable Congruence. As a congruence, Wilson's theorem is $(n - 1)! + 1 \equiv 0 \pmod{n}$ if and only if n is a prime number. In a 1974 paper [2] by M. V. Subbarao (Alberta, Canada), it is stated " ... there is probably no other simple primality condition in the literature in the form of a congruence." However, a remarkable near miss is provided by

$$n\sigma(n) \equiv 2 \pmod{\varphi(n)},$$

where $\sigma(n)$ denotes the sum of the (positive) divisors of n and $\varphi(n)$ is Euler's φ-function, which counts the number of natural numbers $m \leqslant n$ which are relatively prime to n, i.e., for which $(m, n) = 1$. This congruence is satisfied by all the prime numbers and by no composite numbers with the exception of 4, 6, and 22! If n is a prime p, we have $\sigma(n) = p + 1$ and $\varphi(n) = p - 1$, giving

$$n\sigma(n) = p(p + 1) = p^2 + p$$
$$= (p^2 - 1) + (p - 1) + 2 \equiv 2 \;(\text{mod }(p - 1)).$$

We shall shortly give Subbarao's nice proof of the surprising result that the only composite solutions are 4, 6, and 22.

As just observed, $\varphi(p) = p - 1$ for a prime p, implying that

$$n - 1 \equiv 0 \;(\text{mod }\varphi(n)) \text{ for } n \text{ a prime.}$$

At present, no composite solution is known for this congruence, yet we are unable to declare there is none. Another congruence, for which the only composite solution less than 100,000 is $n = 4$, is given by

$$\varphi(n) \cdot t(n) + 2 \equiv 0 \;(\text{mod } n),$$

where $t(n)$ denotes the number of (positive) divisors of n. It is a simple matter to see that it is satisfied by every prime p:

$$\varphi(n) \cdot t(n) + 2 = (p - 1) \cdot 2 + 2 = 2p \equiv 0 \;(\text{mod } p).$$

The conditions on composite solutions of this congruence are the main subject of Subbarao's paper. We conclude this essay with his straightforward investigation of the composite solutions of $n\sigma(n) \equiv 2 \;(\text{mod }\varphi(n))$.

Suppose a composite solution n has the prime decomposition

$$n = 2^a \cdot p_1^{a_1} \cdot p_2^{a_2} \cdots p_r^{a_r}.$$

Subbarao first observes that no index a_i of an odd prime p_i could exceed 1. Using the established formula ([1], page 230)

$$\varphi(n) = 2^{a-1}\big(p_1^{a_1} - p_1^{a_1 - 1}\big)\big(p_2^{a_2} - p_2^{a_2 - 1}\big) \cdots \big(p_r^{a_r} - p_r^{a_r - 1}\big),$$

we see that $a_i \geq 2$ implies that $p_i | \varphi(n)$. Clearly $p_i | n$. Thus $\varphi(n)$ $| n\sigma(n) - 2$ yields $p_i | n\sigma(n) - 2$, and $p_i | 2$, which is impossible for an odd prime. Consequently, each $a_i = 1$ and

$$n = 2^a p_1 p_2 \cdots p_r.$$

If $a \neq 0$, the same argument leads to $2^{a-1} | 2$, implying $2^{a-1} = 1$ or 2 and $a = 1$ or 2. Thus $a = 0, 1,$ or 2.

For $n = 2^a p_1 p_2 \cdots p_r$, in general we have

$$\varphi(n) = 2^{a-1}(p_1 - 1)(p_2 - 1) \cdots (p_r - 1).$$

If $a = 0$, the factor 2^{a-1} simply does not occur. In any case, each of the r factors $(p_i - 1)$ is an even number, implying $2^r | \varphi(n)$. Using a well-known formula for $\sigma(n)$ ([1], page 164) we obtain

$$\sigma(n) = (2^{a+1} - 1)(1 + p_1)(1 + p_2) \cdots (1 + p_r),$$

in which each factor $(1 + p_i)$ is also an even number. Thus $2^r | \sigma(n)$ and the congruence $\varphi(n) | n\sigma(n) - 2$ yields $2^r | 2$, making $r = 0$ or 1. Therefore n is either of the form $n = 2^a$ or $2^a p_1$. Since $a = 0, 1,$ or 2, we have the values $n = 1, 2, 4, p_1, 2p_1,$ and $4p_1$. Being concerned only with composite solutions, we have just $n = 4, 2p_1,$ and $4p_1$.

For $n = 4p_1$, we have $\varphi(n) = 2(p_1 - 1)$, containing a factor 4. Since $4 | n$, our congruence $\varphi(n) | n\sigma(n) - 2$ implies $4 | 2$. Thus we have only $n = 4$ or $2p_1$. For $p_1 = 2$, we have $2p_1 = 4$. Thus the form $n = 2p_1$ encompasses all the composite solutions.

Finally, for $n = 2p_1$ we have

$$n\sigma(n) = 2p_1(1 + 2 + p_1 + 2p_1) = 6p_1(p_1 + 1),$$

and

$$n\sigma(n) - 2 = 6p_1^2 + 6p_1 - 2 = 6(p_1^2 - 1) + 6(p_1 - 1) + 10.$$

Also, $\varphi(n) = 2^0(p_1 - 1) = p_1 - 1$. Consequently, our congruence yields $p_1 - 1 | 10$. This makes $p_1 - 1 = 1, 2, 5,$ or 10, and $p_1 = 2, 3, 6,$ or 11. Since 6 is not a prime, we see that the composite solutions are restricted to $n = 2p_1 = 4, 6,$ or 22. A direct check verifies that each of these is a solution.

Combining this result with an idea we encountered earlier, we see that a simple primality condition is now available in the form

$$n\sigma(n) + \tfrac{1}{2}\left[|B^2 - 1| - (B^2 - 1)\right] \equiv 2 \pmod{\varphi(n)},$$

where $B = (n - 4)(n - 6)(n - 22)$. The value of B is a non-zero integer for all natural numbers n other than 4, 6, and 22. Thus $|B^2 - 1| = B^2 - 1$ for all $n \neq 4$, 6, and 22, making the left side of the above condition congruent to $n\sigma(n)$ in all but these three cases. But, except for $n = 4$, 6, and 22, we have seen that

$$n\sigma(n) \equiv 2 \pmod{\varphi(n)}$$

is a primality condition. And for $n = 4$, 6, and 22, we have $B = 0$, giving

$$n\sigma(n) + \tfrac{1}{2}\left[|B^2 - 1| - (B^2 - 1)\right] \equiv n\sigma(n) + 1$$
$$\equiv 2 + 1 \equiv 3 \pmod{\varphi(n)},$$

failing to satisfy the congruence.

Exercises

1. Prove that no integer d between 1 and 41 divides $f(x) = x^2 + x + 41$, x an integer.
2. Prove that $f(x) = x^2 + x + 41$ is never a square, except for $f(40) = f(-41) = 41^2$.
3. Find 40 consecutive integers x for which $f(x) = x^2 + x + 41$ yields composite numbers exclusively.
4. If $p = p_1^2 + p_2^2 + p_3^2$, where p, p_1, p_2, p_3 are primes, prove that one of p_1, p_2, p_3 is 3.
5. If p is a prime number, prove that $2^p + 3^p$ is never a perfect power.

References

1. W. Sierpinski, Theory of Numbers, Warszawa, 1964.
2. M. V. Subbarao, On two congruences for primality, Pacific J. Math., 52 (1974) 261–268.

CHAPTER 5

TWO COMBINATORIAL PROOFS

In this essay we discuss two theorems which are proven in *Mathematical Gems* (Vol. I). In each case, however, the present treatment is completely independent.

1. Dirac's Theorem on Hamiltonian Circuits. We begin with a brief review of the basic notions involved. A graph is simply a collection of vertices and edges, each edge joining a pair of vertices. In a simple graph there are no "loops" (edges whose endpoints are both the same vertex) and at most one edge joins a pair of vertices. (See Figure 22.) The valence of a vertex is the number of edges which occur at the vertex.

In 1857 the Irish mathematician William Hamilton directed attention to graphs possessing paths and circuits along the edges of the graph which go through every vertex exactly once; see Figure 23. (In a circuit, the two endpoints are the same and a closed cycle results.) Despite the labor of a century, no necessary and sufficient condition is known today for a graph to have a Hamiltonian circuit. In 1952, G. A. Dirac established the following sufficient condition:

A simple graph on n vertices ($n \geqslant 3$), each of valence $\geqslant n/2$, contains a Hamiltonian circuit.

The brilliant proof by the Hungarian prodigy Louis Pósa at the age of 15 (1962) is given in Chapter 2 of *Mathematical Gems* (Vol. 1). Here we consider the delightful 1958 proof by Donald J.

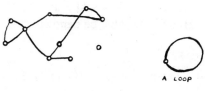

A LOOP

FIG. 22

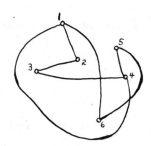

FIG. 23

Newman (Yeshiva University, then of AVCO's Research and Advanced Development Division).

He takes the vertices to represent n people and the presence of an edge AB to indicate that A and B are friends. The theorem, then, is equivalent to the statement that the n people can be seated around a circular table so that everyone sits between two friends. Suppose, to the contrary, that this is impossible to arrange. Newman then introduces some ringers from the local Dale Carnegie Course, people who are everybody's friends. Acceptable seating arrangements now become easier to construct. Clearly n Dale Carnegie types alternated with our n people gives everyone around the table two friendly neighbors. Let k denote the minimum number of Dale Carnegiers that are necessary to permit an acceptable arrangement.

Suppose, in an acceptable plan which employs the minimum number k of "special" guests, the Carnegie man P sits between A and B. Now it would be clearly wasteful to have two Carnegiers together. Thus A and B are from the original group. Also, A and B

cannot be friends, for then P would not be needed between them. Let the places around the table be denoted

$$APBX \ldots \ldots YA.$$

Let T' denote a person who is a friend of T. We show that the combination $A'B'$ (a friend of A followed by a friend of B) cannot occur in the arrangement. Since A, himself, is not a friend of A, the AP at the beginning of our representation does not qualify as an $A'B'$. Similarly PB does not qualify because B is not a B'. Thirdly, BX is not an $A'B'$ because B and A are not friends. At the end, YA is disqualified for the same reason. Now, if somewhere past B there occurred an $A'B'$, we would have

$$APB \ldots . A'B' \ldots A.$$

Reversing the order of those between B and A', inclusive, we get

$$APA' \ldots . BB' \ldots A,$$

an arrangement in which everyone still has a friend on each side. But now we see that P is no longer needed, for he is sitting between two friends. In this case, only $k - 1$ special friends are needed, contradicting the minimality of k. Thus no $A'B'$ can possibly occur in the arrangement

$$APB \ldots \ldots A.$$

The consequence of this is that each friend of A must be followed by a nonfriend of B. Because the valence of each vertex of the given graph is at least $n/2$, each of the original n people has at least $n/2$ friends among themselves. Altogether, then, A has at least $n/2 + k$ friends among the total $n + k$ people. Since each of these A' is followed by a non-B', there must also be at least this same number, $n/2 + k$, of non-B'. Thus we have

$$\text{number of non-}B' > \frac{n}{2} + k,$$

and

$$\text{number of } B' \geqslant \frac{n}{2} + k$$

(every original person has this many friends).

But everybody is either a B' or a non-B'. Adding these inequalities, then, gives the total number of people $n + k \geqslant n + 2k$, which is a contradiction unless $k = 0$.

2. Fermat's Simple Theorem (Chapter 1 of *Mathematical Gems*, Vol. 1). In 1640, the great French number theorist Pierre de Fermat stated the theorem:

If p is a prime number, then, for every integer n, $n^p - n$ is divisible by p.

The theorem embraces all integers n—positive, negative, and zero. In 1956, S. W. Golomb gave the following purely combinatorial proof for the case of positive n (which is the main case).

Suppose we have beads of n different colors, an unlimited supply of each color, and we make up necklaces each containing p beads. First we make all possible straight strings of p beads and then form the necklaces by joining their ends. This leads to many duplicates. Since we are going to count the number of different necklaces, excluding duplicates, we must prescribe exactly how they are to be constructed and compared. The cyclic order of the beads is reversed if the string is wrapped into a necklace by bringing it down from the top rather than up from the bottom. Obviously two necklaces are duplicates if spinning one around produces the other. (See Figure 24.) But we must decide whether or not two necklaces are to be considered the same if one needs to be flipped over before it can be spun into the other. Our decision is not to permit a necklace to be turned over. Accordingly, the two necklaces in Figure 25 are not duplicates. Thus it makes a dif-

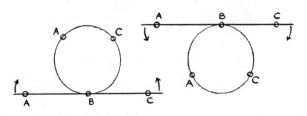

FIG. 24

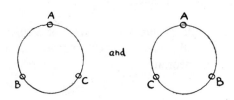

and

FIG. 25

ference how the strings are wrapped into necklaces. We insist that all strings be wrapped the same way (say from the bottom).

Now there are n different choices for the color of each of the p beads on a string. Thus there is a total of

$$n \cdot n \cdot \cdot \cdot n = n^p$$

different strings. Spinning one of the n necklaces whose beads are all the same color produces no variations. Therefore duplicate necklaces occur only among those made from the other $n^p - n$ multi-color strings. We shall show that, excluding the one-color cases, there are exactly p copies of each necklace. Thus the number of distinct necklaces is $(n^p - n)/p$. Being a whole number, this implies p divides $n^p - n$.

We need to establish a p-to-one correspondence between the strings and the necklaces. We do this by starting with a necklace N and showing that it yields p *different* strings when cut at the p places between consecutive beads. (See Figure 26.) Obviously, p strings $s_1, s_2, \ldots, s_p$ arise from the p cuts. The problem is to show

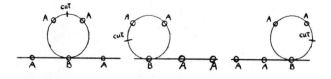

FIG. 26

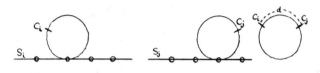

FIG. 27

that they are all different. Suppose, therefore, that some two strings s_i and s_j are the same. Let the number of beads between the cuts C_i and C_j corresponding to these strings be d. (See Figure 27.) If a copy of N is spun around, from the same starting position on top of a second copy of N, through an arc containing d beads, thus bringing the upper C_i on top of the lower C_j, and a double cut made at this point, the identical strings s_i and s_j are produced. Thus the spin through d beads could not have altered the colors in any way since the ones on top are still the same as the corresponding beads underneath. In N, then, every bead must be the same as the one d places around from it. If $d = 1$, all the beads are the same color. Since the n necklaces of this type are not under consideration, we have $d > 1$. We note also that, being the number of beads between two different cuts, $d < p$.

Now a spin through a complete revolution of p beads carries N into itself, as does a spin through d beads. Since p is a prime and $1 < d < p$, d does not divide into p. Suppose $p = qd + r$, where $0 < r < d$. (See Figure 28.) Then q spins through d beads leaves a spin through r beads to complete a spin of a whole revolution. This smaller spin through r beads still carries N into itself, and therefore it must be that every rth bead around N is the same color. Now $r \neq 1$, lest all beads be the same color. Thus $1 < r$

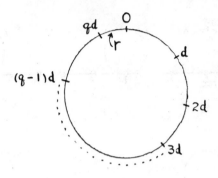

$< d < p$. Now similar considerations show the existence of a smaller number $r_1 > 1$ with the same property ($1 < r_1 < r < p$). Repeated applications of this argument show the existence of an unlimited number of positive integers r_i in the range $1 < r_i < p$. Clearly this is impossible, and the theorem follows.

(Since n^p and n are always of the same parity, we see that $n^p - n$ is always divisible by $2p$ whenever p and 2 are different.)

Exercises

1. What is the greatest number of acute angles that can occur in a convex n-gon?

2. Prove that if p is a prime number exceeding 5, then p divides some integer whose decimal representation is a string of 1's.

3. Show that if at no vertex of a simple polyhedron do exactly three edges meet, then at least eight of the faces are triangles.

4. Show that the total number of permutations of n different things, taken any number at a time, is $[n!e]$, where $[x]$ denotes the greatest integer not exceeding x.

5. A regular $(2n + 1)$-gon is inscribed in a circle. What is the probability that the triangle formed by three vertices chosen at random contains the center? (This is problem #3 on the Second U.S.A. Mathematical Olympiad, 1973.)

References

1. D. J. Newman, A problem in graph theory, Amer. Math. Monthly, 65 (1958) 611.

2. S. W. Golomb, Combinatorial proof of Fermat's "Little" Theorem, Amer. Math. Monthly, 63 (1956) 718.

CHAPTER 6

BICENTRIC POLYGONS, STEINER CHAINS, AND THE HEXLET

1. Bicentric Polygons. Every triangle has an incircle $I(r)$ (i.e., center I and radius r) and a circumcircle $O(R)$. Conversely, it is natural to ask when a given pair of nested circles are the incircle and circumcircle of a triangle. (See Figure 29.) This old problem was solved by the great Euler (1707–1783). Denoting by s the distance between the centers I and O of the circles, he found that

$$R^2 = s^2 + 2Rr$$

if and only if $I(r)$ and $O(R)$ are the incircle and circumcircle of a triangle. However, given two suitable circles, appropriately placed, we still have a problem in determining the triangle itself. The length of a tangent to the inner circle varies from point to point around the outer one. To obtain the triangle in question, we want to find the particular point A on $O(R)$ from which three successive tangents (AB, BC, CA) bring us back around again to the starting point A. The surprising thing is that any point on $O(R)$ may be used as starting point! That is to say, if two circles permit successive tangents to close a triangle for one starting point A on a circle $O(R)$, then they do so for all starting points on the circle. (The proofs of these results are given in the Appendix.)

Now triangles are well behaved, always having both an incircle and a circumcircle. Quadrilaterals may have both, one, or neither (Figure 30). Polygons which have both an incircle and a circumcircle are called *bicentric*. In 1798, Nicholaus Fuss (1755–1826), a student and friend of Euler, characterized the bicentric polygons

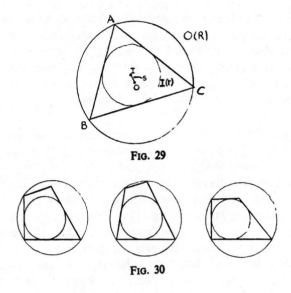

FIG. 29

FIG. 30

with 4, 5, 6, 7, and 8 sides. For quadrilaterals, the circles must satisfy

$$2r^2(R^2 - s^2) = (R^2 - s^2)^2 - 4r^2s^2.$$

But the interesting result here is again that if the circles permit successive tangents to close a quadrilateral for one starting point on the outer circle, then they do so for all points on this circle. Jean-Victor Poncelet (1788–1867), the French genius who laid the

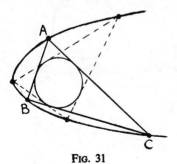

FIG. 31

foundations of projective geometry while languishing in a Russian prisoner-of-war camp (he was one of Napoleon's soldiers in his disastrous Moscow campaign), showed that the same result is true for polygons with any number of sides. In fact, Poncelet proved the remarkable result that the same is true for any two given conics, not just a pair of circles! (See Figure 31.)

2. Steiner Chains. Now suppose that a circle A is given inside a circle B. Let C be a circle which is tangent to both A and B. Let $D, E, \ldots$, denote links in a chain of circles, each tangent to A and B, and to the adjacent circles in the chain (Figure 32). Such a series of circles is called a Steiner Chain in honor of the outstanding Swiss geometer Jacob Steiner (1796–1867). It may or may not happen that the Steiner chain forms a perfectly closed ring around A. It is natural to expect that everything depends on where the first circle C is placed. Here again, however, the fact is that if a Steiner chain closes for one starting circle, then it closes no matter where the chain is begun. An elegant proof of this can be based on circular inversion. The figure is inverted in a circle which causes A and B to be carried into concentric circles A' and B' (this is always possible to arrange). This transformation carries the circles of the chain into a chain of equal circles between A' and B' (Figure 33). If these equal images close a chain in the annulus between A' and B', clearly it does not matter where the chain is

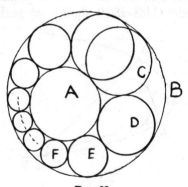

Fig. 32

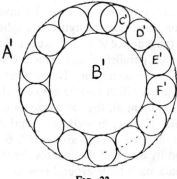

FIG. 33

begun. The conclusion follows the observation that the image chain closes if and only if the object chain closes between A and B.

We observe also that if the image chain goes around the annulus n times before closing, the same will happen for the object chain. Some chains, however, never close.

3. The Hexlet. In 1936, Frederick Soddy (1877–1956), a Chemistry Professor at Oxford (who is famous for his pioneering work on isotopes and for an original approach to economics), considered a three-dimensional analog of a Steiner chain.

He began with three mutually tangent spheres A, B, C, admittedly a somewhat specialized configuration. These form a little ring of spheres with a hole in the middle. A chain of spheres D, E, . . . , is constructed to touch each of A, B, C and also their neighbors in the chain. The chain threads through the hole in the A-B-C ring and interlocks with it. From our experience with Steiner chains, we suspect that *if* the chain of spheres closes into a necklace for some placing of the first sphere, it will close for every choice of first sphere. Surprisingly, there is no if about it—for every set of mutually tangent spheres A, B, C, every chain closes into a necklace no matter where the first sphere is begun. And, to our astonishment, in every necklace there occur exactly six spheres! Thus the name "hexlet."

The reason for this is again made clear by inversion, this time "spherical" inversion. Inverting the figure in a sphere which has as center the point of tangency of A and B, we see that the images A' and B' are a pair of parallel planes which contain the image sphere C' tangentially between them. The spheres of the chain are transformed into spheres which also lie between A' and B', touching them. This makes them all the same size as C'. Since each of these spheres touches C', too, as well as A' and B', the image of the chain is a chain of equal spheres around C'. But any sphere C' is precisely enclosed by a ring of six spheres the same size as itself (think of six golf balls on a table around one in the middle).

H. S. M. Coxeter, the distinguished Canadian geometer, has reported on this subject in a paper entitled "Interlocking Rings of Spheres," Scripta Mathematica, 1952, Vol. 18, p. 113. Here he treats a general theorem which was stated without proof by Jacob Steiner and proven in 1938 by Louis Kollros:

For every ring containing p spheres, there exists a ring of q spheres, each touching each of the p spheres, where $(1/p) + (1/q) = \frac{1}{2}$.

Soddy's Hexlet is the special case given by $p = 3$. (This makes $(1/3) + (1/q) = \frac{1}{2}$, implying $q = 6$.)

APPENDIX

1. *To Prove* $R^2 = s^2 + 2Rr$.

Let CI, OI extended give the points D, E, F (Figure 34) on $O(R)$. Then

$$DI \cdot IC = EI \cdot IF$$

$$= (R - s)(R + s)$$

$$= R^2 - s^2,$$

or

$$R^2 = s^2 + DI \cdot IC.$$

It remains only to show that $DI \cdot IC = 2Rr$.

It turns out that $\angle DAI = \angle DIA$ (each equals $\frac{1}{2} \angle C + \frac{1}{2} \angle A$), making $\triangle DAI$ isosceles and $DA = DI$. Now $O(R)$ is also the circumcircle of $\triangle ADC$. By the formula for the circumradius of a triangle, we thus have

$$R = \frac{AD}{2 \sin \dfrac{C}{2}}, \quad \text{that is}, \ AD = DI = 2R \sin \frac{C}{2}.$$

But from right triangle ITC, we have $r/IC = \sin(C/2)$, giving $IC = r/\sin(C/2)$. Thus

$$DI \cdot IC = 2R \sin \frac{C}{2} \cdot \frac{r}{\sin \dfrac{C}{2}} = 2Rr,$$

as required.

2. *To prove that if a triangle closes for one starting point C on* $O(R)$, *then it does so for all points on* $O(R)$.

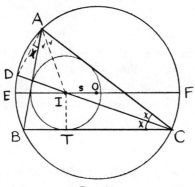

Fig. 34

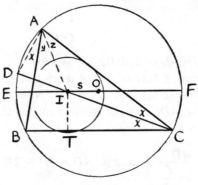

FIG. 35

Let us pick any point C on $O(R)$ and draw tangents CA and CB (Figure 35) to $I(r)$. We want to prove that the side AB thus determined is also a tangent to $I(r)$. The situation is almost the same as it was in proving Euler's result. Because CA and CB are tangents, CI does bisect $\angle C$. Let IT be perpendicular to CB. Hence, we again have

$$IC = \frac{r}{\sin \dfrac{C}{2}} .$$

Also, $O(R)$ still circumscribes $\triangle ADC$, so that

$$AD = 2R \sin \frac{C}{2} .$$

Also again we have $DI \cdot IC = EI \cdot IF = (R - s)(R + s) = R^2 - s^2$. But we know that $R^2 - s^2 = 2Rr$ (since the triangle closes for some starting point, this follows by result 1 above). Hence we get

$$DI \cdot IC = 2Rr.$$

That is,

$$DI \cdot \frac{r}{\sin \dfrac{C}{2}} = 2Rr, \quad \text{or } DI = 2R \sin \frac{C}{2} .$$

This means that $DI = AD$, again making $\angle DAI = \angle DIA$. Referring to Figure 35, we have $\angle DIA = x + y$. But $\angle DIA$ is an exterior angle to $\triangle AIC$, and is accordingly $x + z$. Hence $y = z$, and AI does indeed bisect $\angle A$. This implies that I is the incenter of $\triangle ABC$ and $I(IT)$ the incircle. Thus AB is tangent to $I(r)$.

References

1. H. Dorrie, 100 Great Problems of Elementary Mathematics, Dover, New York, 1965.
2. C. S. Ogilvy, Excursions in Geometry, Oxford University Press, New York, 1969.

CHAPTER 7

A THEOREM OF GABRIEL LAMÉ

Euclid's algorithm for calculating the greatest common divisor of two numbers is well covered in many elementary textbooks. Applied to 154 and 56 it yields the number 14:

$$154 = 2 \cdot 56 + 42,$$
$$56 = 1 \cdot 42 + 14,$$
$$42 = 3 \cdot 14.$$

I can remember reading somewhere years ago that the French mathematician Gabriel Lamé had proved in 1844 that the number of steps (i.e., divisions) in an application of the Euclidean algorithm never exceeds 5 times the number of digits in the lesser number. Having wondered about this now and again for a long time, I was delighted recently to run across a beautiful proof by H. Grossman in the American Mathematical Monthly, Volume 31, 1924, page 443. Later I discovered the same proof in Sierpinski's outstanding *Theory of Numbers* [2].

Suppose a_n is the lesser number in a pair (a_{n+1}, a_n) for which the Euclidean algorithm contains n steps ($n > 1$). We focus our attention on the least possible value of a_n (for a given value of n). Let the n steps in the process be represented by

$$a_{n+1} = m_n \cdot a_n + a_{n-1}, \qquad (0 < a_{n-1} < a_n)$$
$$a_n = m_{n-1} \cdot a_{n-1} + a_{n-2}, \qquad (0 < a_{n-2} < a_{n-1})$$
$$\cdots\cdots\cdots\cdots\cdots\cdots\cdots\cdots\cdots\cdots\cdots\cdots$$
$$a_4 = m_3 \cdot a_3 + a_2, \qquad (0 < a_2 < a_3)$$
$$a_3 = m_2 \cdot a_2 + a_1, \qquad (0 < a_1 < a_2)$$
$$a_2 = m_1 \cdot a_1.$$

Since the numbers involved are all natural numbers, each is at least 1. We note in particular, however, that $m_1 \neq 1$, lest the last line reduce to $a_2 = a_1$ in violation of the preceding line which contains the condition (0 is $< a_1 < a_2$). Consequently, the least m_1 is 2. Accordingly (working backwards through the representation),

$$a_1 \geqslant 1, \text{ and}$$

$$a_2 \geqslant 2 \cdot 1 = 2,$$

$$a_3 \geqslant 1 \cdot 2 + 1 = 3,$$

$$a_4 \geqslant 1 \cdot 3 + 2 = 5,$$

$$a_5 \geqslant 1 \cdot 5 + 3 = 8,$$

and so on. Calculating on the minimal basis of $m_i = 1$ for $i > 1$, we see in general that a_n is at least as great as f_n, where f_n is the nth term of the Fibonacci sequence $1, 2, 3, 5, 8, 13, 21, \ldots$, defined by $f_1 = 1$, $f_2 = 2$, and for $n > 2$, $f_n = f_{n-1} + f_{n-2}$.

For this sequence it is easy to show that $f_{n+5} > 10 \cdot f_n$. By direct inspection we see that the claim is valid for $n = 1, 2, 3$. For $n > 3$, we have

$$f_n = f_{n-1} + f_{n-2} = 2f_{n-2} + f_{n-3},$$

while

$$f_{n+5} = f_{n+4} + f_{n+3} = 2f_{n+3} + f_{n+2}$$

$$= 3f_{n+2} + 2f_{n+1} = 5f_{n+1} + 3f_n$$

$$= 8f_n + 5f_{n-1} = 13f_{n-1} + 8f_{n-2}$$

$$= 21f_{n-2} + 13f_{n-3}$$

$$> 20f_{n-2} + 10f_{n-3}$$

$$= 10f_n.$$

From this we see that f_{n+5} has at least one more digit than f_n. Now a look at the sequence shows that for $0 < n \leqslant 5$, f_n has 1 digit. By the result just proved, then,

$$\text{for } 5 < n \leqslant 2 \cdot 5, \qquad f_n \text{ has at least 2 digits,}$$
$$\text{for } 2 \cdot 5 < n \leqslant 3 \cdot 5, \qquad f_n \text{ has at least 3 digits,}$$
$$\text{for } 3 \cdot 5 < n \leqslant 4 \cdot 5, \qquad f_n \text{ has at least 4 digits,}$$
$$\cdots\cdots\cdots\cdots\cdots\cdots\cdots\cdots\cdots\cdots$$
$$\text{for } k \cdot 5 < n \leqslant (k+1) \cdot 5, \qquad f_n \text{ has at least } k+1 \text{ digits,}$$
$$\cdots\cdots\cdots\cdots\cdots\cdots\cdots\cdots\cdots\cdots$$

Consider now any natural number n. For some integer k we have $k \cdot 5 < n \leqslant (k+1) \cdot 5$. Thus f_n has at least $k+1$ digits. Since $a_n \geqslant f_n$, then a_n, too, has at least $k+1$ digits. Accordingly, 5 times the number of digits in a_n is at least $5(k+1)$. Hence

$$n \leqslant (k+1) \cdot 5 \leqslant 5 \text{ times the number of digits in } a_n,$$

establishing the theorem.

We conclude with the observation that the number 5 in this theorem is the "best possible" in that the theorem is false for every lesser integer (see Exercise 5).

Exercises

While the following exercises except #5 cannot claim to bear on the particular topic of this essay, they are very nice elementary problems in the general subject of number theory.

1. What is the least number containing only 1's which is divisible by the number 33 .. 3 which contains 100 3's?

2. If $d_1 = 1$, $d_2, \ldots, d_k = n$ are the positive divisors of the natural number n, show that $(d_1 d_2 \cdots d_k)^2 = n^k$.

3. (a) Find 3 different natural numbers, relatively prime in pairs, such that the sum of any two is divisible by the third.

  (b) Find 3 different natural numbers such that the product of any two leaves a remainder of 1 upon division by the third.

4. Solve $a^3 - b^3 - c^3 = 3abc$, $a^2 = 2(b + c)$ in natural numbers.

5. Prove that 5 is "best possible" in this theorem of Lamé.

References

1. Uspensky and Heaslett, Elementary Number Theory, McGraw-Hill, New York, 1939, p. 43.
2. W. Sierpinski, Theory of Numbers, Warszawa (1964) 21–22.

CHAPTER 8

BOX-PACKING PROBLEMS

In addition to the packing of three-dimensional boxes with solid blocks, we shall consider the covering of two-dimensional regions with plane figures. Surprisingly, there is even a beautiful theorem about packing a line with intervals.

1. Packings in the Plane.

(a) *Polyominoes.* One of the pioneers in this field is Solomon Golomb (University of Southern California). In 1953, while a student at Harvard, he directed attention to plane packings of "polyominoes"—figures obtained by joining unit squares together along their edges in rook-wise fashion (a chess rook could travel through all the squares in the piece). There are not many ways to connect 2, 3, or 4 squares; we get only 1 domino, 2 trominoes, and 5 tetrominoes (see Figure 36). There are 12 pentominoes (Figure 37) and 35 hexominoes, but no general formula is known for the number of "n-ominoes" which can be made from n squares. We note that for greater n ($\geqslant 7$) it is not permitted to form a piece with a "hole" in it.

(i) Since chess and checkers are so common, their 8×8 board is a popular two-dimensional box for packing polyominoes. It is a trivial matter to pack 32 dominoes in a checkerboard. However, it is mildly surprising to learn that it is impossible to pack 31 dominoes into a checkerboard from which a pair of opposite corners has been removed (see Figure 38). We are led to this conclusion quickly and easily by the coloring scheme on a check-

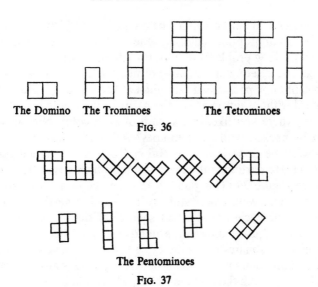

The Domino   The Trominoes   The Tetrominoes

FIG. 36

The Pentominoes

FIG. 37

erboard. Each domino, covering two adjacent squares, must cover one square of each color. Accordingly, any region which is covered by a collection of dominoes will possess the same number of white squares as black squares. Since opposite corners are the same color, our reduced board does not enjoy this critical equality

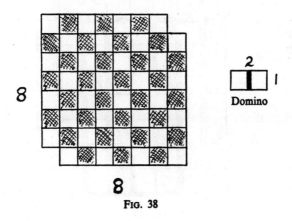

8

8

2

1

Domino

FIG. 38

of colors, and therefore cannot be packed with dominoes. As we shall see, an appropriate coloring scheme is central to the solution of many packing problems in both two and three dimensions.

Of course, deleting any squares of just one color leaves a region which cannot be packed with dominoes. Accordingly, let us reduce the board without throwing off the parity of the colors by deleting, from anywhere you like, one square of each color. Now can the region be packed with 31 dominoes? A beautiful proof that this can always be done is due to Ralph Gomory, a mathematician with IBM. He partitions the board by introducing two "forks," as shown in Figure 39. This puts all the squares in a cycle, around which one can walk again and again. We observe that adjacent squares in the cycle are adjacent squares of the board. Thus the colors of the squares alternate around the cycle. Because of this, the number of squares along the cycle between two squares A and B of different colors is always even. That is, there is always exactly enough room along the cycle to fit in a whole number of dominoes between a deleted black square A and a deleted white one B. The only problem is to fit them in around the corners of the cycle. But there is no difficulty here since the dominoes can be turned to run

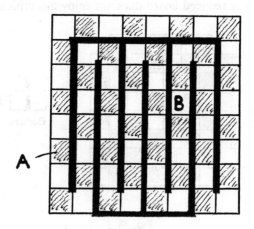

Fig. 39

across or up-and-down the board. Packing the two paths of the cycle between A and B thus covers the reduced board.

(ii) We turn now to two problems discussed by Golomb in his paper "Checker Boards and Polyominoes" (American Mathematical Monthly, Volume 61, 1954, pages 675–682). In 1965, Golomb published a book *Polyominoes* (Scribners), which is a treasure of material on this topic.

Since each tromino has an area of 3 units, a checkerboard has room for 21 of them with one square left over. It is easy to see that a checkerboard can be covered with 21 *L*-trominoes and 1 mono-mino (see Figure 40). It doesn't even matter where the monomino is placed to start things off. Clearly it must go into one of the four quarters of the board, and, indeed, into one of the quarters of that quarter. An *L*-tromino, then, just completes the 16th of the board in which the monomino is placed. A second *L*-tromino can be placed to have a square in each of the other three 16ths in that quarter of the board, the covering of each of which is also completed with another *L*-tromino. The next tromino is placed around the completed quarter so as to occupy one square of each of the other three quarters, and it remains only to finish each of these quarters as the first one was done.

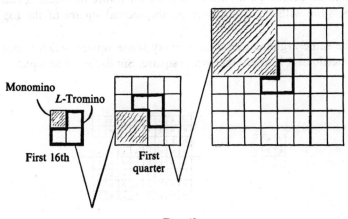

Monomino

L-Tromino

First 16th

First quarter

Fɪɢ. 40

It is quite a different matter to cover a checkerboard with 21 straight trominoes and 1 monomino. Golomb's answer to this is to color the squares with three colors—red, white, and blue—by repeating the basic pattern D (Figure 41), across and down the board (disregarding overhanging parts). The important property of this arrangement is that no matter where a straight tromino is placed it occupies a square of each of the three colors. We immediately see this to be so for a tromino placed to coincide with a row or column of a copy of D. However, a tromino which is placed to extend across two copies of D always picks up from the one copy exactly the colors it misses in the other. The 21 trominoes, then, will cover 21 squares of each color. But a direct count reveals that there are only 21 red squares and only 21 blue squares. Thus the trominoes must occupy all the red and all the blue squares, and also 21 of the 22 white squares. The monomino, then, is forced to be placed on a white square.

Let us try the monomino in the white square which is the second square in the top row in Figure 42. If it were possible to pack around this the 21 straight trominoes, then the same arrangement, reflected in the midline XY, would permit a packing of the checkerboard with the monomino placed in the second square of the bottom row. But this is a blue square, and we know that the monomino cannot go on a blue square. Therefore no packing can be possible with the monomino on the second square of the top row.

The same argument eliminates every white square which is not symmetric in XY to another white square. Similarly, an acceptable

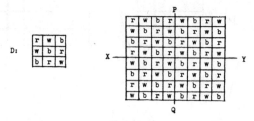

FIG. 41

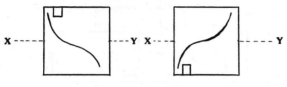

FIG. 42

white square must be symmetric to another white square in the other midline PQ, too. Thus, while the L-tromino permitted the monomino to be put anywhere, the straight tromino requires that it go only in the third square of the third row (or in the equivalent images in XY and PQ). With this discovery, an actual packing is easily found (see Figure 43).

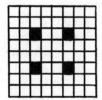 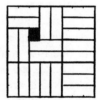

FIG. 43

(iii) Using another clever coloring scheme of Golomb's, David Klarner proved a surprising fact about the L-tetromino. One can see from Figure 44 that there is no difficulty in packing a 4×6 rectangle with L-tetrominoes. However, try as you will, there is no way to pack a 10×10 rectangle with pieces of this type. This is a consequence of the following theorem:

THEOREM. *Rectangles which can be packed with L-tetrominoes always need an even number of them to do it.*

Proof. Suppose an $a \times b$ rectangle can be packed with L-tetrominoes. Since each piece has area 4 units, the total area ab

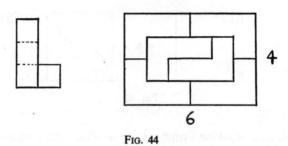

FIG. 44

must be a multiple of 4. Consequently, not both a and b can be odd. For definiteness, suppose that the base b is even. Then the rectangle contains an even number of columns of squares, and these entire columns can be colored alternately black and white. The beauty of this scheme is that no matter where an L-tetromino is placed on the rectangle, it covers 3 squares of one color and 1 of the other. Considering any particular packing of the rectangle, suppose that the number of pieces which cover 3 black squares and 1 white one is x, and that the number which cover 3 white squares and 1 black one is y. (See Figure 45.) The total number of black squares which are covered is then $3x + y$, and the total number of white squares is $x + 3y$, But these numbers are each $ab/2$, since all the squares are covered and half are each color

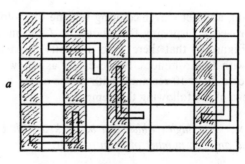

b (even)

FIG. 45

because b is even. Thus we have

$$3x + y = x + 3y, \quad 2x = 2y, \quad \text{and} \quad x = y.$$

Accordingly, the number of pieces used, which is $x + y$, is $2x$, an even number.

Therefore it is hopeless to try packing a 10×10 rectangle (which would take 25 copies). Because the number of L-tetrominoes, $ab/4$, is an even number, we see that ab must be a multiple of 8. It can be shown that *the L-tetromino packs an $a \times b$ rectangle if and only if $a, b > 1$ and 8 divides ab.* In 1965, D. W. Walkup proved the similar result: *The T-tetromino packs an $a \times b$ rectangle if and only if 4 divides each of a and b.*

A polyomino, like the L-tetromino, which uses an even number of copies in every rectangle it packs, is called an "even" polyomino. If even one rectangle exists which is packable with an odd number of copies, a polyomino is said to be "odd." In the exercises we ask that it be established that there exist an infinity of (dissimilar) even and an infinity of (dissimilar) odd polyominoes.

(iv) Our final item on polyominoes is a simple proof by Golomb that the family of the 35 hexominoes, each used once, cannot be assembled to form a rectangle. We proceed indirectly. Any rectangle which they pack would have area $35 \times 6 = 210$, an even number. Coloring the rectangle in checkerboard fashion would provide 105 squares of each color. Now the hexominoes divide into two groups according to their shapes:

(i) the 24 hexominoes which cover, on a checkerboard, 3 squares of each color (Figure 46);

(ii) the 11 hexominoes which cover 2 squares of one color and 4 of the other (Figure 47).

In packing the hexominoes of group (i), we cover ($24 \times 3 = 72$) an even number of squares of each color. While we do not know the exact number of (say) black squares which the members of group (ii) will cover, we can conclude that, being the sum of 11 even numbers (either 2's or 4's), it will also be an even number. (Similarly for the other color.) Altogether, then, however the whole

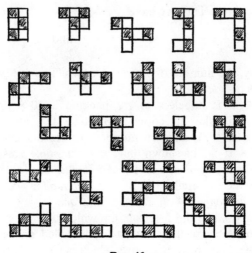

FIG. 46

The 24 hexominoes of group (i)

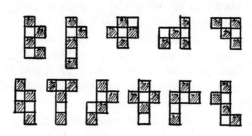

FIG. 47

The 11 hexominoes of group (ii)

family may be packed, it will cover an even number of squares of each color (the sum of two even numbers), not the required 105.

(b) *Stained-Glass Windows.* Pictured in Figure 48 is a portion of an infinite stained-glass window with the engaging property that, wherever it is viewed through a 3 × 4 rectangle (the 3 vertical and the 4 horizontal), one sees precisely 3 orange squares, 4 yellow squares, and 5 red squares. Such a window is obtained simply by

r	y	o	y	r	y	o	y	r	y	o
y	r	r	o	y	r	r	o	y	r	r
r	o	y	r	r	o	y	r	r	o	y
r	y	o	y	r	y	o	y	r	y	o
y	r	r	o	y	r	r	o	y	r	r
r	o	y	r	r	o	y	r	r	o	y
r	y	o	y	r	y	o	y	r	y	o
y	r	r	o	y	r	r	o	y	r	r

FIG. 48

repeating throughout the plane a 3 × 4 rectangle which is colored according to the desired prescription. In general an $m \times n$ rectangle and any prescription of colors may be used. Wherever the window is viewed, one can imagine that the 3 × 4 rectangle has been shifted to that position from some specified initial position by sliding it across the plane and then up or down as required. Clearly, as the rectangle is moved, the colors it loses at one edge are precisely the colors it gains at the opposite edge. If the rectangle is turned to become a 4 × 3 viewing frame (the 4 vertical and the 3 horizontal), our window loses its magic property. However, there are infinite stained glass windows that give constant results no matter which way the viewing rectangle is used. Some windows even possess the property when viewed through a non-rectangular frame, such as a "cross." In a joint paper with the young Dutch mathematician M. L. J. Hautus, Professor Klarner gives the theory of constructing the most general kind of window in which it is impossible to detect the method of construction by inspection of the finished product.

Golomb's three-coloring of the checkerboard (Figure 41) is a typical application of stained-glass windows. Using the window generated by repeating the basic $n \times n$ square D (Figure 49), Klarner established that:

An $a \times b$ rectangle R can be packed with $1 \times n$ strips if and only if n divides a or n divides b.

1	2	3	-	-	n
n	1	2	-	-	n-1
n-1	n	1	-	-	n-2
-	-	-	-	-	- -
-	-	-	-	-	- -
2	3	4	-	-	1

D:

FIG. 49

Each row and column is a cyclic permutation of $1, 2, \ldots, n$ and the
1's occur along the main diagonal.

(See the exercises.) An easy corollary to this is the following
general result:

THEOREM. *An $a \times b$ rectangle R can be packed with $c \times d$
rectangles if and only if either* (i) *each of c, d divides one of a, b,
each a different one, or* (ii) *both c and d divide the same one of a, b,
say a, and the other (b) is of the form $b = cx + dy$, for some
nonnegative integers x and y.*

This theorem shows the fundamental role of trivial packings
(repeated rows and columns). If a rectangle R can be packed with
a rectangle K in any way at all, then a packing of R can be
accomplished either by packing the whole thing trivially (condition (i) or by packing trivially two abutting subrectangles (condition (ii)). (See Figures 50 and 51.)

Condition (i): c divides a, and d divides b.

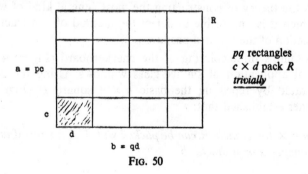

pq rectangles
$c \times d$ pack R
trivially

$a = pc$

c

d

$b = qd$

FIG. 50

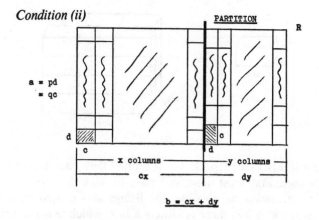

Condition (ii)

FIG. 51

x columns with base c and y columns with base d pack R

2. Solid Packings.

(a) *De Bruijn's Theorem.* The problem of packing bricks into boxes leads to unexpectedly interesting results. The 7-year old son of the prominent Dutch mathematician N. G. de Bruijn (rhymes with coin) discovered one day that he couldn't pack his $1 \times 2 \times 4$ bricks into his little $6 \times 6 \times 6$ box. This led de Bruijn to consider the matter and in 1969 he published the following theorem about harmonic bricks, that is, bricks with dimensions $a \times ab \times abc$.

THEOREM. *A box can be packed with the harmonic brick $a \times ab \times abc$ if and only if the box has dimensions $ap \times abq \times abcr$ for some natural numbers p, q, r (i.e., if the box is a "multiple" of the brick).*

A moment's reflection reveals that an $ap \times abq \times abcr$ box can be packed trivially with $a \times ab \times abc$ bricks. (See Figure 52.) Klarner's result of the previous section (concerning the packing of an $a \times b$ rectangle with $1 \times n$ strips) is a special case of the two-dimensional version of de Bruijn's theorem. However, the impact of de Bruijn's theorem is that the *only* boxes which

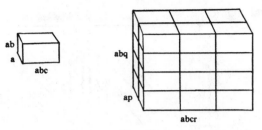

FIG. 52

harmonic bricks can pack are the ones they can pack trivially. While there may exist nontrivial ways to pack the box, the trivial way must always be possible. De Bruijn also proved that, for a nonharmonic brick, there is always a box, which is *not* a multiple of the brick, that it packs.

Now harmonic bricks include many common sizes—$1 \times 2 \times 4$, $1 \times 1 \times 2$, $1 \times 2 \times 2$, etc. Thus de Bruijn's theorem provides some interesting surprises. For example, there is no way to pack a $10 \times 10 \times 10$ box with $1 \times 2 \times 4$ bricks because 10 is not divisible by 4. In fact, a $10 \times 10 \times 10$ box cannot even be packed with the more versatile $1 \times 1 \times 4$ brick, which is called the straight tetracube. While this, too, is an immediate consequence of de Bruijn's theorem, we consider two independent proofs of it. The first of these involves a novel way of constructing a three-dimensional stained-glass window.

Let a corner of the box and the three edges which meet there be taken as the origin and the (positive) axes of a system of cartesian coordinates. (See Figure 53.) We associate with each of the unit cubes of the box the coordinates (x, y, z) of the corner closest to the origin. Now each unit cube is colored with one of the four colors 1, 2, 3, 4 according as the number $x + y + z$ is congruent (mod 4) to 1, 2, 3, or 4. It follows easily that wherever a $1 \times 1 \times 4$ brick is packed in the box, it occupies one unit cube of each color. Consequently, the box is not packable unless it has the same number (250) of cubes of each color. The fact is, there are only 249 cubes colored 3, implying the box is unpackable. It is a nice exercise in permutations and combinations to deduce this number of cubes colored 3. However, it is derived more easily as follows.

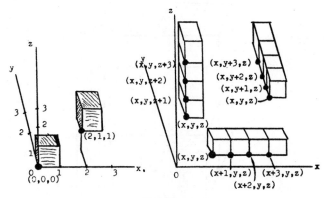

FIG. 53

Standing $1 \times 1 \times 4$ bricks on end we can trivially pack the bottom 4 layers of the box. Repeating this procedure, we can pack the next 4 layers too. By running bricks the other ways, it is a simple matter to pack the rest of the box except a $2 \times 2 \times 2$ region in one corner (say opposite the origin). Because each brick occupies a cube of each color, the colors in the part which we have packed must occur with the same frequency (248 times, since there are only 8 more cubes left). However, a direct investigation of the remaining $2 \times 2 \times 2$ piece shows that the color 3 occurs there only once more (in the cube $(9, 9, 9)$). (See Figure 54.)

Our second proof comes from Brian Lapcevic, a high school teacher from Metropolitan Toronto, Ontario. The $10 \times 10 \times 10$ box contains, in a trivial arrangement, 125 blocks of size $2 \times 2 \times 2$. These are colored alternately black and white as shown in Figure 55. Clearly, no matter where a $1 \times 1 \times 4$ block is placed in the box, it must occupy two unit cubes of each color. Thus the packing is possible only if the box contains the same number of black and white unit cubes. Since there is an odd number (125) of $2 \times 2 \times 2$ sections, the colors cannot occur with the same frequency, implying the packing is hopeless.

De Bruijn's theorem brings to mind a startling result concerning the decomposition of a rectangle into squares of which no two are the same size. This subject was taken up in 1936 by four students

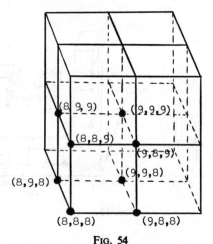

FIG. 54
Each of x, y, z is either an 8 or a 9; every arrangement of 8's and 9's occurs.

from Trinity College, Cambridge—Brooks, Smith, Stone, and Tutte. Since that time many such decompositions have been discovered. (See Figure 56.) However, it was a great surprise to learn that if a rectangle cannot be decomposed trivially into *equal* squares, then it cannot be decomposed into squares in any way whatsoever!

(b) *Prime and Composite Boxes.* Sometimes one is able to accomplish the packing of a box B by packing a collection A of

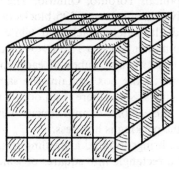

FIG. 55

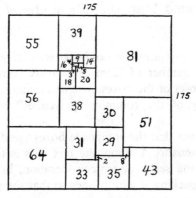

FIG. 56

smaller ones and then packing *B* with the filled boxes of *A* (multiple copies of the smaller boxes being permitted, of course). If there is no such set *A* of smaller, packable boxes, then *B* is said to be a "prime" box relative to the set of boxes *S* which are packable with the blocks under consideration. (Clearly, if *S* contains one box, then copies of this box can be arranged to form an endless string of bigger packable boxes, implying *S* is infinite.) For example, the $1 \times 2 \times 4$ box is prime with respect to the boxes packable with the *L*-tetracube, but it is "composite" relative to those packable with the straight tetracube. (See Figure 57.)

In 1969, Dr. Klarner and F. Gobel proved a general theorem about infinite sets of boxes which have integral dimensions, whether or not the set arises as a set of boxes packable with blocks.

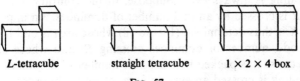

L-tetracube   straight tetracube $1 \times 2 \times 4$ box

FIG. 57

THE BOX-PACKING THEOREM.   *The number of prime boxes is always finite.*

That is to say, in any infinite set of boxes with integral dimensions, all but a finite number of them are merely combinations of a certain finite subset of the boxes. The determination of the prime boxes for many of the common "polycubes" is still an open question.

Now it turns out that the composite boxes are distinguished by a simple characteristic. A composite box B is not only packable with primes of the set S under consideration, but there always exists a way of packing B with primes so that the packing can be cleft in two by a plane which slices down through B without cutting through any of the prime boxes in the packing. Thus a composite box can always be packed by packing separately two smaller boxes whose union gives the full packing of it. Applying this to the sets S of boxes which are packable with blocks, we see that a box is composite if and only if there exists a packing of it with the *blocks* (rather than smaller boxes) which, likewise, has "cleavage." Thus it is not necessary to know all the primes which are smaller than a given box B in order to decide the nature of B. It can be classified as prime or composite by examining just its own packings of the prescribed blocks, without reference to the other boxes in S. For example, it is possible to pack an $8 \times 11 \times 21$ box with 44 copies of a $2 \times 3 \times 7$ brick, but in no packing does there occur a cleaving plane, showing the box to be a prime. We conclude this section with a simple proof that the 6×6 box is so highly composite in the set of boxes which are packable with 1×2 dominoes that every packing of it has cleavage.

First of all, draw the 10 lines which rule the box into its 36 unit squares. We shall show that the number of dominoes which cross a given ruling is always even. Suppose, to the contrary, that some ruling R is crossed by an odd number of dominoes. An impossible region K is thus determined (Figure 58) whose area is odd because of the odd number of dominoes crossing R, and whose area is even because it is packed with a whole number of dominoes. Thus every ruling is crossed an even number of times. In order to cross

all 10 rulings a positive even number of times, a minimum of
10(2) = 20 dominoes is required (if a ruling is crossed at all, it
must be crossed at least twice). But a domino can cross only one
ruling. This means that at least 20 dominoes are needed to cross
all the rulings and eliminate cleavage. However, the 6 × 6 box has
room for only 18 dominoes 1 × 2.

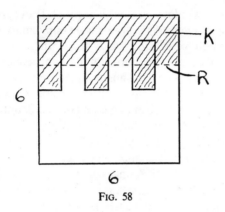

Fig. 58

(c) *The Puzzles of Slothouber-Graatsma and Conway.* Finally we
have arrived at the puzzles which I started to write about in this
essay. Their theories are basically the same, each employing the
same 3-dimensional version of a stained-glass window. The first
puzzle occurs in a book written by the Dutch architects Jan
Slothouber and William Graatsma.

(1) *The Slothouber-Graatsma Puzzle.* It is required to assemble
six 1 × 2 × 2 blocks and three 1 × 1 × 1 blocks into a 3 × 3 × 3
cube (Figure 59). This is an easy puzzle and many people can do it
in a short time without formulating any firm theory. However, its
theory is very attractive and it has the advantage of applying to
more complicated situations.

Consider the 3-dimensional stained-glass window obtained by
repeating the 2 × 2 × 2 cube *D* which has its 8 unit cubes colored
with the colors 1, 2, 3, 4 as illustrated in Figure 60. This induces
the following coloring of the unit cells in a 3 × 3 × 3 cube which

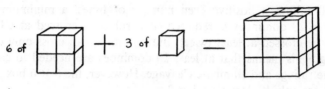

FIG. 59

is placed in the "window" so that a copy of D occurs in its back, lower left corner (Figure 61). Now it is a simple matter to check by direct observation of all the cases that, wherever a $1 \times 2 \times 2$ block may be packed in the cube, its four unit cubes occupy cells which are one of each color. Thus the placement of the six blocks of this type will fill 6 unit cubes of each color. However, a direct count reveals that there are only 6 cells colored 2, only 6 colored 3, and only 6 colored 4. Thus the $1 \times 2 \times 2$ blocks must occupy all the cells colored 2, 3, 4, as well as 6 of the 9 cells colored 1. As a result, the $1 \times 1 \times 1$ blocks must be placed in positions colored 1.

Now no 3×3 layer of 9 unit cubes can be filled completely with just $1 \times 2 \times 2$ blocks, because the number of unit cells of a layer which such a block occupies is either 4 (if it's "flat" in the layer) or 2 (if "on end"), and no sum of 2's and 4's is the odd number 9. Thus each of the nine layers of the cube must contain a $1 \times 1 \times 1$ block. In the second layer from the bottom, then, there

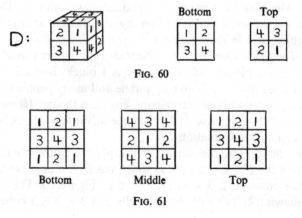

FIG. 60

FIG. 61

is no choice but to put a $1 \times 1 \times 1$ block in the middle, which is actually the center cell of the whole cube.

In the top layer, a $1 \times 1 \times 1$ block must go in a corner (it doesn't matter which one because the cube can be spun around to move a designated corner to any of the 4 corner positions). In order to have a $1 \times 1 \times 1$ block in every slice, the remaining $1 \times 1 \times 1$ block is forced to go opposite the one in the top layer. Armed with the knowledge that the three $1 \times 1 \times 1$ blocks must occupy a diagonal, we can construct the cube with a minimum of experimentation. (See Figure 62.)

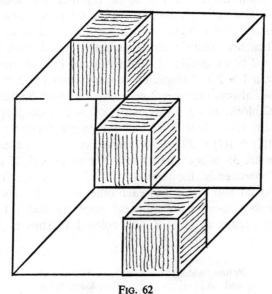

Fig. 62
The Slothouber-Graatsma Puzzle

(2) *Conway's Puzzle.* In Conway's puzzle a $5 \times 5 \times 5$ cube is to be constructed from 13 blocks $1 \times 2 \times 4$, 1 block $2 \times 2 \times 2$, 1 block $1 \times 2 \times 2$, and 3 blocks $1 \times 1 \times 3$. (See Figure 63.) This really good puzzle is the invention of John Conway, a prominent

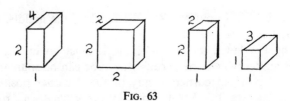

Fig. 63

English mathematician from Cambridge. It is more complicated than the Slothouber-Graatsma puzzle, but it is not overly difficult.

Its mathematical analysis parallels the theory of the Slothouber-Graatsma puzzle. The same 3-dimensional stained-glass window (derived from the $2 \times 2 \times 2$ block D) that was used in the Slothouber-Graatsma puzzle induces the following coloring (Figure 64) in a $5 \times 5 \times 5$ cube which has a copy of D in its back, lower left corner. Again, a direct inspection reveals that, wherever a $1 \times 2 \times 2$ block occurs, it occupies a cell of each color. Consequently, a $1 \times 2 \times 4$ block, being simply two $1 \times 2 \times 2$ blocks end-to-end, always occupies 2 cells of each color. Similarly for a $2 \times 2 \times 2$ block, which is just two $1 \times 2 \times 2$ blocks side-by-side. Collectively, then, these blocks of the puzzle occupy a total of $13(2) + 1(2) + 1(1) = 29$ cells of each color. A direct count shows that there are 35 cells colored 1 and 30 cells of each of the other colors. Consequently, the three $1 \times 1 \times 3$ blocks must occupy 6 cells colored 1 and one cell of each other color. We observe that no two cells colored 1 are adjacent, implying that a $1 \times 1 \times 3$ block can occupy at most 2 cells colored 1. Thus each of the

Bottom, middle, and top layers				
1	2	1	2	1
3	4	3	4	3
1	2	1	2	1
3	4	3	4	3
1	2	1	2	1

Second and fourth layers				
4	3	4	3	4
2	1	2	1	2
4	3	4	3	4
2	1	2	1	2
4	3	4	3	4

Fig. 64

$1 \times 1 \times 3$ blocks must occupy 2 cells colored 1, lest they fall short of the required total of 6 such cells. These blocks, then, must occupy three consecutive cells with colors $(1, 2, 1)$, $(1, 3, 1)$, and $(1, 4, 1)$.

We observe that the blocks $1 \times 2 \times 4$, $2 \times 2 \times 2$, and $1 \times 2 \times 2$ each contribute an even number of cells to any layer in which they are involved. Thus these blocks are called the "even" blocks, and the $1 \times 1 \times 3$ block is called "odd." Since there is an odd number of cells in every 5×5 layer, each layer must contain a cell (perhaps all three) of an odd block. From this we see immediately that there must occur an odd block parallel to each edge of the cube (consider the 5 layers from back to front: if no odd block runs from back to front, then at most 3 of these layers could contain a cell of an odd block). With the following two additional results we are able to solve the puzzle (their easy proofs are left as an exercise):

   (i) No odd block can be placed so that it lies entirely in a "middle" layer (e.g., from left to right).
  (ii) Not all three odd blocks can be placed completely in the surface layers of the cube (so as to avoid the $3 \times 3 \times 3$ core). In fact, one odd block must be placed entirely in the core. (Studying the induced coloring, we see that it is highly restrictive to be obliged to place the odd blocks in positions colored $(1, 2, 1)$, $(1, 3, 1)$, and $(1, 4, 1)$.)

Now we can deduce that the three odd blocks are forced to "snake" through the cube as illustrated in Figure 65. From the coloring, it is evident that the odd block in the $3 \times 3 \times 3$ core must occupy an edge of the core. We may suppose this edge to be the bottom left one which runs from front to back, for the cube could be so turned if constructed otherwise. Thus, as shown, every solution to the puzzle can be turned to have an odd block running from front to back on the left of center in the second layer from the bottom.

The remaining odd blocks must pierce the front and back layers. Their directions imply that each lies entirely in the layer of this pair that it pierces. In order to get all the layers from top to

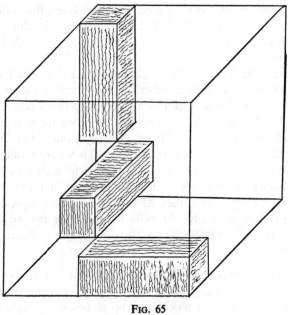

FIG. 65
Conway's Puzzle

bottom pierced, the vertical block must reside in the top 3 layers, and the other block must run horizontally in the bottom. In order to pierce all the layers from left to right, this latter block must remain in the 3 right-hand layers, forcing the vertical block to the left face. Thus, except for deciding which one will go at the front and which at the back, their positions are fixed. Since these alternatives give equivalent results, there is essentially only one way to place the three odd blocks. With its secret discovered, the puzzle goes together very easily.

Professor Klarner has discovered that 25 Y-pentacubes (Figure 66) also pack a $5 \times 5 \times 5$ cube. Around Waterloo, we refer to the problem of doing this as "Klarner's Puzzle." It took him about 45 minutes to find a packing, while an electronic computer failed to do so in an hour. However, with a little "coaching," the computer soon turned up nearly 400 different solutions. (See the exercises.)

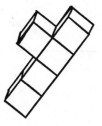

FIG. 66
The Y-Pentacube

(d) *Related Results.* Many results have been discovered concerning the boxes which are packable with various polycubes. The list in Table 67 is far from complete. The names are starred to distinguish them from plane polyominoes. $\langle a \times b \times c \rangle$ denotes the box $a \times b \times c$; $P(X)$ denotes the set of prime boxes for the polycube X; $B(X)$ denotes the set of boxes packable with X.

TABLE 67

	V_3^*	$\{\langle 1 \times 2 \times 3 \rangle, \langle 1 \times 5 \times 9 \rangle, \langle 3 \times 3 \times 3 \rangle\} = P(V_3^*)$
	L_4^*	$\{\langle 1 \times 2 \times 4 \rangle, \langle 1 \times 3 \times 8 \rangle, \langle 2 \times 2 \times 6 \rangle, \langle 2 \times 3 \times 6 \rangle, \langle 2 \times 3 \times 4 \rangle\} = P(L_4^*)$
	T_4^*	$\{\langle 1 \times 4 \times 4 \rangle, \langle 3 \times 3 \times 8 \rangle\} \subseteq P(T_4^*)$

TABLE 67 (*Continued*)

	$N_4{}^*$	$\{\langle 2 \times 3 \times 4 \rangle, \langle 2 \times 4 \times 4 \rangle, \langle 2 \times 4 \times 5 \rangle\} \subseteq P(N_4{}^*)$
	$L_5{}^*$	$\{\langle 1 \times 2 \times 5 \rangle, \langle 1 \times 9 \times 15 \rangle, \langle 3 \times 5 \times 5 \rangle\} \subseteq P(L_5{}^*)$
	$Y_5{}^*$	$\{\langle 2 \times 5 \times 6 \rangle, \langle 3 \times 4 \times 5 \rangle, \langle 2 \times 4 \times 10 \rangle, \langle 2 \times 5 \times 8 \rangle,$ $\langle 4 \times 4 \times 5 \rangle, \langle 2 \times 5 \times 11 \rangle, \langle 4 \times 5 \times 5 \rangle, \langle 2 \times 4 \times 15 \rangle,$ $\langle 5 \times 5 \times 5 \rangle, \langle 2 \times 5 \times 13 \rangle, \langle 2 \times 5 \times 15 \rangle\} \subseteq P(Y_5{}^*)$
	$N_5{}^*$	$\{\langle 2 \times 4 \times 5 \rangle, \langle 2 \times 5 \times 5 \rangle, \langle 2 \times 5 \times 6 \rangle, \langle 2 \times 5 \times 7 \rangle\}$ $\subseteq P(N_5{}^*),$ $\langle 3 \times 5 \times 14 \rangle \in B(N_5{}^*)$
	$V_5{}^*$	$\{\langle 3 \times 5 \times 6 \rangle, \langle 4 \times 5 \times 6 \rangle, \langle 4 \times 4 \times 10 \rangle,$ $\langle 4 \times 5 \times 10 \rangle\} \subseteq P(V_5{}^*)$
	$F_5{}^*$	$\langle 4 \times 5 \times 10 \rangle \in P(F_5{}^*)$

82

TABLE 67 (*Continued*)

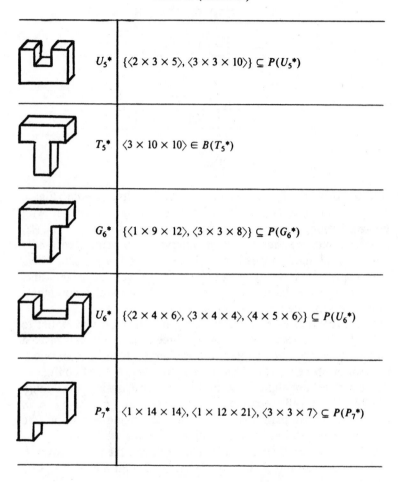

	U_5^*	$\{\langle 2 \times 3 \times 5 \rangle, \langle 3 \times 3 \times 10 \rangle\} \subseteq P(U_5^*)$
	T_5^*	$\langle 3 \times 10 \times 10 \rangle \in B(T_5^*)$
	G_6^*	$\{\langle 1 \times 9 \times 12 \rangle, \langle 3 \times 3 \times 8 \rangle\} \subseteq P(G_6^*)$
	U_6^*	$\{\langle 2 \times 4 \times 6 \rangle, \langle 3 \times 4 \times 4 \rangle, \langle 4 \times 5 \times 6 \rangle\} \subseteq P(U_6^*)$
	P_7^*	$\langle 1 \times 14 \times 14 \rangle, \langle 1 \times 12 \times 21 \rangle, \langle 3 \times 3 \times 7 \rangle \subseteq P(P_7^*)$

3. Packing the Line. We conclude this essay with a theorem about packing a line with intervals. Consider an infinite line L of unit squares, and a configuration A consisting of two unit squares which, while having corresponding points 3 units apart, are con-

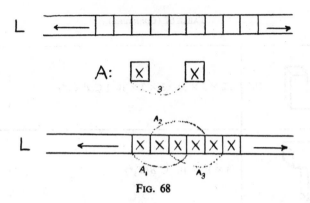

Fig. 68

sidered to be rigidly connected with an invisible handle (Figure 68). It is desired to fill all the cells of L by covering it with nonoverlapping copies of A. Clearly, three copies of A (A_1, A_2, A_3) can be fitted together to fill an interval of 6 cells. Repeatedly doing this along L covers it completely. It is a trivial result, then, that copies of any 2-cell configuration A can pack the line. (Throughout the discussion, we consider the cells of a configuration to be separated by integral distances.)

In the realm of 3-cell configurations, it is also a trivial matter to cover L with a piece A in which the three cells are equally spaced "a" units apart ("a" copies fit together to form a continuous interval of $3a$ cells). (See Figure 69.) However, a 3-cell configuration which is "unbalanced" is another matter. Consider the configuration A with cells separated by distances a and b, where $a < b$. Of course, we are permitted to turn over the rigid piece to put the cells in reverse order. In this position let us denote the configuration by the letter B (Figure 70). The problem, then is to cover L with copies of A and B. The surprising fact is that it can always be done!

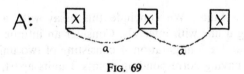

Fig. 69

A:

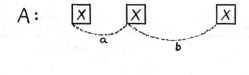

B:

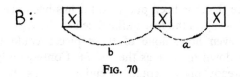

FIG. 70

THEOREM. *Any 3-cell configuration packs the line.*

Proof. We choose any cell O on L at which to start, and we show how to fill in the right half of L. The same procedure applied to the left half completes the task.

The technique is to work our way along L to the right from O by putting in copies $A_1, A_2, \ldots ,$ of A until one won't fit. Clearly we can put these in until the gap between the first two cells of A_1 are all filled (starting A_1 at O). See Figure 71. Formally, our general procedure is to begin a copy of A at the first unfilled cell to the right of O. In the event that a copy of A will not fit at some step, we put in a copy of B instead. An endless unbroken interval is thus built up to the right of O. The theorem is established, then, by proving that B always fits whenever A doesn't.

We have observed already that no difficulty can occur in placing the first "a" copies of A. Thus at least the first $a + 1$ cells must be filled by the time we need to resort to using a B (the filled-in first gap of A_1 together with the end-cells of this gap give an unbroken string of $a + 1$ cells).

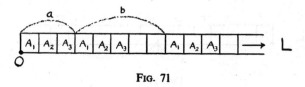

FIG. 71

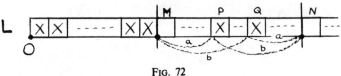

Fig. 72

Let us suppose that, at some cell M, A won't fit and neither will B. Every piece that has been put in so far has been placed so that its initial cell occupies the *first* unfilled cell to the right of O. Since M is empty even now, none of these pieces could have been started as far down the line as the cell M. Consequently, none of the pieces already placed could extend as far as the square N which is $a + b$ units (i.e., the length of a piece) beyond M. Thus N must be empty.

We see, then, that M and N are both empty. These cells would be able to accept the endcells of either A or B. Since neither fits in at M, it must be because their middle cells are blocked. Thus the cells P and Q which are between M and N and, respectively, "a" units from them, must both be occupied. (P because A won't fit, and Q because B won't.) Now we consider how the cell Q could have come to be occupied already.

Since Q is beyond M, it could not be occupied by the initial cell of a piece. If it were occupied by the middle cell of a B, then its final cell would occupy N (contradiction), and if by the middle cell of an A, its final cell would project beyond N (impossible). Thus Q must be filled by the final cell of a piece.

The piece cannot be an A, for then its middle cell would occupy M, which is still empty. Thus it must be a B. The first cell of this piece would be a cell T which is "a" units to the left of M. At the time of inserting this piece B, the cells T and Q must have been empty in order to accept it. However, M has always been empty.

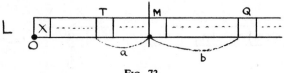

Fig. 73

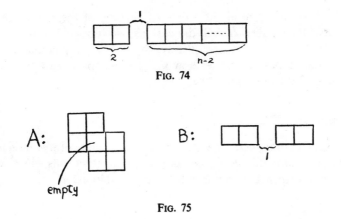

FIG. 74

FIG. 75

Accordingly, an A would have fitted in at T-M-Q, and we would never have had occasion to resort to putting in a B. This contradicts the assumption that a B was so used, implying that Q must be unoccupied. Thus a B will fit in at M-Q-N, a contradiction which completes the proof. (See Figure 73.)

We observe that 3 is the greatest value of n for which we can say "every n-cell configuration packs the line." For $n > 3$, the n-cell configuration consisting of two continuous intervals of 2 and $n-2$ cells which are separated by a distance of 1 unit obviously fails to pack the line (Figure 74).

Corresponding to the matter of packing the line is the problem of packing an infinite checkerboard with copies of a rigidly connected configuration of unit squares, that is, of packing the plane. The 6-cell configuration A shown in Figure 75 clearly fails to pack the plane. However, the 4-cell configuration B does pack the plane (see exercise 5). Don Coppersmith, a mathematician with IBM, claims that every 4-cell configuration packs the plane, and it is conjectured that every 5-cell configuration will also do it. The following general proposition has been proved:

If every k-cell configuration in n-dimensional space packs n-dimensional space, then, for $m > n$ also, every k-cell configuration in m-dimensional space packs m-dimensional space.

Thus our theorem about the 3-cell packing of the line extends through the spaces of all dimensions; so does Coppersmith's theorem (for $m > 1$). Consequently, copies of a piece containing 3 (or 4) unit cubes, no matter how scattered in space, can pack the whole of 3-dimensional space!

Exercises

1. The pentominoes are known to pack each of the regions given in Figure 76, the blacked-out cells indicating cells which are to remain empty. Determine a packing for each region.

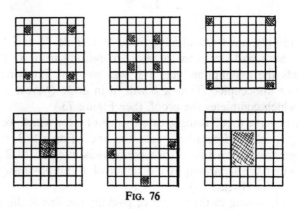

FIG. 76

2. Prove that there is an infinity of dissimilar even polyominoes and also an infinity of dissimilar odd polyominoes.

3. Prove Klarner's Theorem: *An a × b rectangle can be packed with 1 × n strips if and only if n divides a or n divides b.* Apply this result to prove the theorem which follows it on page 68.

4. Make 25 *Y*-pentacubes and solve Klarner's puzzle of assembling them into a $5 \times 5 \times 5$ cube.

5. Determine a scheme for tiling the plane with copies of

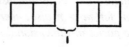

6. Try to find a 5-cell configuration which does not pack the plane; an 8-cell configuration which does not pack 3-space. These are open questions.

References

1. N. G. de Bruijn, Filling boxes with bricks, Amer. Math. Monthly, 76 (1969) 37–40.
2. D. A. Klarner, Packing a rectangle with congruent n-ominoes, J. Combinatorial Theory, 7 (1969) 107–115.
3. D. A. Klarner and F. Gobel, Packing boxes with congruent figures, Indag. Math., 31 (1969) 465–472.
4. J. Slothouber and W. Graatsma, Cubics, Octopus Press, Deventer, The Netherlands, 1970.
5. G. Katona and D. Szasz, Matching problems, J. Combinatorial Theory, Series B, 10 (1971) 60–92.
6. S. W. Golomb, Polyominoes, Scribners, New York, 1965.
7. D. W. Walkup, Covering a rectangle with T-tetrominoes, Amer. Math. Monthly, 72 (1965) 986–988.
8. C. J. Bouwkamp and D. A. Klarner, Packing a box with Y-pentacubes, J. Recreational Math., 1973.
9. D. A. Klarner and M. L. J. Hautus, Uniformly coloured stained-glass windows, Proc. London Math. Soc., Third Series, 23 (1971) 613–628.
10. D. A. Klarner, A packing theory, J. Combinatorial Theory, 8 (1970) 273–278.
11. M. Gardner, Mathematical games, Scientific American, 214 (1966) 115.

CHAPTER 9

A THEOREM OF BANG AND THE
ISOSCELES TETRAHEDRON

1. Solid geometry pays as much attention to the tetrahedron as plane geometry does to the triangle. Yet many elementary properties of the tetrahedron are not very well known. Solid geometry is often a more complicated subject than plane geometry, for it is undoubtedly more difficult for the mind's eye to establish and maintain a constant picture of the relative positions of objects in three-dimensional space. Flat figures are much easier to think about and to describe to others. Thus the pursuit of solid geometry generally demands extra motivation. Consequently, I hasten to announce that our little story in this field will not be a burden to our visual imaginations.

2. A particular kind of tetrahedron that arises in many contexts is the isosceles tetrahedron. A tetrahedron $ABCD$ (Figure 77) is isosceles if the members of each pair of opposite edges are equal —$AB = CD$, $AC = BD$, and $AD = BC$. It follows immediately that the faces of an isosceles tetrahedron are all congruent triangles. Thus the faces all have the same perimeter and the same area. Two of our main interests are nice proofs of the somewhat surprising converse theorems:

The only way for all the faces of a tetrahedron to have the same perimeter, or to have the same area, is for them to be fully congruent.

We shall show that equal perimeters, or equal areas, implies the tetrahedron is isosceles, from which the conclusion follows. The

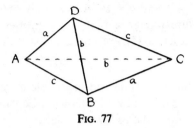

FIG. 77

theorem on perimeters is almost immediate, while the theorem on areas is based on a Theorem of Bang.

3. THEOREM.   *If the faces of a tetrahedron all have the same perimeter, they are congruent.*

Proof.   Let the pairs of opposite edges have lengths a and a', b and b', c and c' (Figure 78). For faces with the same perimeters, we have

$$a + b + c = a + b' + c' = a' + b + c' = a' + b' + c. \quad (*)$$

Cancelling a from the first two parts and a' from the other two, we obtain

$$b + c = b' + c' \quad \text{and} \quad b + c' = b' + c.$$

The first of these gives $b - b' = c' - c$, and the second gives $b - b' = c - c'$. Hence $c' - c = c - c'$, implying $c = c'$, which,

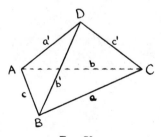

FIG. 78

in turn, yields $b = b'$ and $a = a'$. Accordingly, $ABCD$ is isosceles. We note for future reference that six quantities a, b, c, a', b', c' which are related as in (*) are equal in pairs ($a = a', b = b', c = c'$).

4. It is sometimes possible and profitable to reduce a problem in solid geometry to one in two dimensions. Consider, for example, how easy it is to prove the following result:

A tetrahedron is isosceles if and only if the sum of the face angles at each vertex is 180°.

Taking the tetrahedron $ABCD$ to be hollow, it is cut along the three edges that occur at some vertex, say D, and flattened out (Figure 79). In general, one obtains a hexagon $D_1AD_2CD_3B$. However, if the sum of the face angles at each vertex is 180°, the angles in the hexagon at A, B, C are straight angles. The result, then, is a triangle $D_1D_2D_3$ which has A, B, and C as the midpoints of the sides. Accordingly $AB = \frac{1}{2} D_2D_3 = D_2C = DC$, the opposite edge of the tetrahedron. Similarly, the other two pairs of opposite edges are equal, and the tetrahedron is isosceles.

Conversely, we have seen already that an isosceles tetrahedron has congruent faces. In this case, the face angles at a vertex occur again in the opposite face. Thus their sum is 180° (Figure 80).

In the Spring of 1972, 100 of the best high school mathematics students competed in the first U.S.A. Mathematical Olympiad. The second of the five problems which were posed required one to

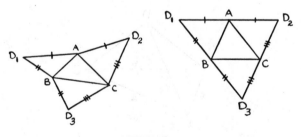

Fig. 79

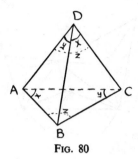

Fig. 80

prove that the faces of an isosceles tetrahedron are acute-angled triangles. As we have seen, the face angles at a vertex of an isosceles tetrahedron add up to 180°. Now every introductory text in solid geometry contains the standard theorem that the sum of two face angles at a vertex of any tetrahedron exceeds the third face angle at that vertex. Thus no face angle, of three whose sum is 180°, could be as great as a right angle. Conversely, however, acute-angled faces do not force a tetrahedron to be isosceles.

5. Next we turn to a theorem that was conjectured by Bang in 1897 and proved in the same year by Gehrke.

BANG'S THEOREM.   *The lines drawn to the vertices of a face of a tetrahedron from the point of contact of the face with the inscribed sphere form three angles at the point of contact which are the same three angles in each face.*

Proof.   Let the tetrahedron be flattened out as described above, and let X and Y, respectively, denote the points of contact in the faces ABC and ACD (Figure 81). Since all the tangents to a sphere from a point are the same length, we have $AX = AY$ and $CX = CY$. Because the side AC is common, the triangles AXC and AYC are congruent, yielding equal angles AXC and AYC opposite the edge AC. Similar considerations involving the other edges of $ABCD$ give six pairs of equal angles which we denote a, b, c, a', b', c', as shown (Figure 82). At the points of contact, we have

$$360° = a + b + c = a + b' + c' = a' + b + c' = a' + b' + c.$$

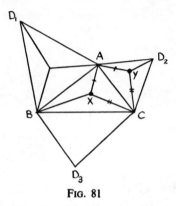

FIG. 81

Thus, according to relation (*), we have $a = a'$, $b = b'$, and $c = c'$, establishing the theorem.

6. Now we are able to complete the theorem:

If all the faces of a tetrahedron have the same area, then they are congruent.

Proof. Instead of using a, b, c, a', b', c' to denote angles as in the proof of Bang's theorem, let us momentarily use them to

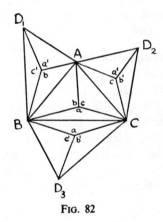

FIG. 82

denote the area of the little triangles in which they occur (see Figure 82). This is permissible since the two little triangles which contain the same symbol are in fact congruent. Since the faces are given to have the same areas, we have

$$a + b + c = a + b' + c' = a' + b + c' = a' + b' + c.$$

Again, according to relation (*), we have $a = a'$, $b = b'$, and $c = c'$. Thus the twelve little triangles go together into three sets of equal quadruples.

Now let the letters A, B, C, D denote also the length of a tangent from the respective vertex A, B, C, D to the inscribed sphere. Then, from the equality of the areas of the triangles which contain the angles a and a', we get

$$\tfrac{1}{2} \cdot B \cdot C \cdot \sin a = \tfrac{1}{2} \cdot A \cdot D \cdot \sin a'.$$

(The area of a triangle with sides x and y and contained angle θ is $\tfrac{1}{2} xy \sin \theta$.) Since the angles a and a' are equal, this reduces to

$$B \cdot C = A \cdot D.$$

Similarly, the other equal quadruples yield $A \cdot B = C \cdot D$ and $A \cdot C = B \cdot D$. Hence

$$\frac{A \cdot B}{B \cdot C} = \frac{C \cdot D}{A \cdot D}, \quad \text{giving } \frac{A}{C} = \frac{C}{A}, A^2 = C^2,$$

and, since A and C are positive, $A = C$. Then $B \cdot C = A \cdot D$ yields $B = D$. Finally, $A \cdot C = B \cdot D$ gives $A^2 = B^2$, leading to $A = B$, and

$$A = B = C = D.$$

These equal tangents imply that the little triangles containing the equal angles a and a' are congruent (SAS). Opposite the equal angles a and a' in these triangles we have equal sides, implying the equality of a pair of opposite edges of the tetrahedron (AD and BC). Similarly for the other opposite pairs, and the tetrahedron is isosceles.

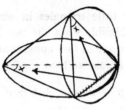

FIG. 83

7. We conclude our story with the theorem that *a tetrahedron is isosceles if and only if its inscribed and circumscribed spheres are concentric.*

Suppose the spheres are concentric. Let $I(R)$ (that is, center I, radius R) denote the circumsphere and $I(r)$ denote the insphere. Now a plane cutting through a sphere has a circular intersection with the sphere and it divides the sphere into two segments. Because our spheres are concentric, the plane of a face of the tetrahedron slices from the circumsphere a segment of height $R - r$, the same for each face. Thus the circles of intersection of the circumsphere and the planes of the faces are all the same size. This simply means that the circumcircles of the triangular faces are all the same size. Since an edge of the tetrahedron borders two faces, it is a chord in two of these equal circumcircles (Figure 83).

Accordingly, the angles subtended by the edge at the other two vertices of the tetrahedron must be the same. Consequently, the

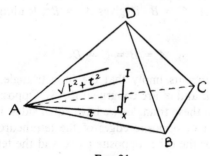

FIG. 84

face angles at a vertex are the angles in the opposite face. Therefore their sum is 180°, and by a previous theorem, the tetrahedron
is isosceles.

Conversely, the congruent faces of an isosceles tetrahedron have
the same area. Thus, as we proved in the immediately preceding
theorem, the length t of a tangent from a vertex to the insphere
$I(r)$ is the same for all the vertices. By the Pythagorean theorem,
then, the distance from I to each vertex is

$$\sqrt{r^2 + t^2} \ .$$

Consequently, the sphere $I(\sqrt{r^2 + t^2})$, passing through all the
vertices, is the circumsphere, implying that I is also the circumcenter (Figure 84).

Exercise

1. $ABCD$ is a regular tetrahedron, and P and Q are two interior
points. Prove that $\angle PAQ$ is less than 60°. (This is Problem #1
from the second U.S.A Mathematical Olympiad, 1973.)

Reference

1. B. H. Brown, Theorem of Bang; Isosceles Tetrahedra; Amer. Math. Monthly,
33 (1926) 224.

CHAPTER 10

AN INTRIGUING SERIES

1. It must have been one of the great surprises in mathematics to discover that the harmonic series diverges. This is seen quickly and easily as follows.

$$1 + \frac{1}{2} + \frac{1}{3} + \frac{1}{4} + \frac{1}{5} + \frac{1}{6} + \frac{1}{7} + \frac{1}{8} + \cdots + \frac{1}{n} + \cdots$$

$$= \left(1 + \frac{1}{2} + \frac{1}{3} + \cdots + \frac{1}{9}\right) + \left(\frac{1}{10} + \frac{1}{11} + \cdots + \frac{1}{99}\right)$$

$$+ \left(\frac{1}{100} + \frac{1}{101} + \cdots + \frac{1}{999}\right) + \cdots$$

$$> \left(\frac{1}{10} + \frac{1}{10} + \cdots + \frac{1}{10}\right) + \left(\frac{1}{100} + \frac{1}{100} + \cdots + \frac{1}{100}\right)$$

$$+ \left(\frac{1}{1000} + \frac{1}{1000} + \cdots + \frac{1}{1000}\right) + \cdots$$

$$= \frac{9}{10} + \frac{90}{100} + \frac{900}{1000} + \cdots$$

$$= \frac{9}{10} + \frac{9}{10} + \frac{9}{10} + \cdots.$$

In this series there is a term corresponding to each natural number n. If all the terms of the series with *composite* denominators are deleted, a drastic reduction is effected and the resulting series is

$$1 + \frac{1}{2} + \frac{1}{3} + \frac{1}{5} + \frac{1}{7} + \frac{1}{11} + \cdots,$$

containing, beyond 1, only the reciprocals of the prime numbers. It must have come as a second surprise to learn that even this severely depleted result is still divergent. (An interesting proof of this is given in my little book *Ingenuity in Mathematics*, Vol. 23, *New Mathematical Library*, Mathematical Association of America.) Our interest in this short essay is the series obtained from the harmonic series upon the deletion of all the terms which contain the digit 9:

$$1 + \frac{1}{2} + \cdots + \frac{1}{8} + \frac{1}{10} + \cdots + \frac{1}{18} + \frac{1}{20}$$
$$+ \cdots + \frac{1}{88} + \frac{1}{100} + \cdots + \frac{1}{108} + \frac{1}{110} + \cdots .$$

Since this reduction seems to leave a richer series than the previous thinning of the harmonic series, our third surprise is that this series does converge. This was proven in 1914 by A. J. Kempner of the University of Illinois. It is a nice application of induction.

First of all, the powers of 10 may be used to divide the terms into groups as follows:

$$\left(1 + \frac{1}{2} + \cdots + \frac{1}{8} \right) + \left(\frac{1}{10} + \cdots + \frac{1}{88} \right)$$
$$+ \left(\frac{1}{100} + \cdots + \frac{1}{888} \right) + \cdots .$$

Denoting the sum of the nth group by a_n, we may write the series

$$a_1 + a_2 + \cdots + a_n + \cdots .$$

The first and greatest fraction in the group a_n is $1/10^{n-1}$. We shall show that there are fewer than 9^n fractions in the group a_n, implying that the value of a_n is less than $9^n/10^{n-1}$. Convergence then follows easily.

A direct check reveals that there are 8 fractions in a_1, and 72 in a_2, establishing fewer than 9^n terms in a_n for $n = 1$ and 2. Let us take as our induction hypothesis that a_k contains fewer than 9^k fractions for all $k = 1, 2, \ldots, n$. Consider, then, the group a_{n+1}.

This group contains $1/10^n$ and all the undeleted fractions between $1/10^n$ and $1/10^{n+1}$. Since every fraction has numerator 1, let us work just with the denominators. The range from 0 to 10^{n+1} is 10 times as great as the range from 0 to 10^n. From 10^n to 10^{n+1}, then, there are 9 intervals the size of the one from 0 to 10^n. They are marked by the numbers $10^n, 2 \cdot 10^n, \ldots, 9 \cdot 10^n$.

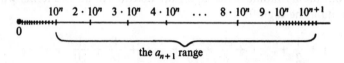

the a_{n+1} range

Since all the numbers in the last section ($9 \cdot 10^n$ to 10^{n+1}) begin with 9, all the corresponding fractions are deleted. Consequently, we need to count the number of denominators remaining in the first 8 sections from 10^n up to $9 \cdot 10^n$. Now, in each of these sections, the denominators which are deleted correspond precisely to those which are deleted from the initial range from 0 to 10^n. Clearly, if the denominator $xy \ldots z$ is deleted from the range 0 to 10^n, then $1xy \ldots z, 2xy \ldots z, \ldots, 8xy \ldots z$ are deleted, respectively, from the sections 10^n to $2 \cdot 10^n, 2 \cdot 10^n$ to $3 \cdot 10^n, \ldots, 8 \cdot 10^n$ to $9 \cdot 10^n$ (if $xy \ldots z$ contains a 9, then they all do). And if $xy \ldots z$ is not deleted from 0 to 10^n, then the corresponding denominators in the other sections will likewise not contain a 9, and will not be deleted either. The number of terms remaining in each of these 8 sections, then, is the same as the number remaining between 0 and 10^n. While we cannot name the exact number, we know by the induction hypothesis that the number is *less than*

$$9 + 9^2 + 9^3 + \cdots + 9^n$$

(*fewer* than 9 for a_1, fewer than 9^2 for a_2, etc.). Accordingly, the number of fractions in a_{n+1}

$$< 8(9 + 9^2 + \cdots + 9^n) = 8 \cdot \frac{9(9^n - 1)}{9 - 1} = 9^{n+1} - 9 < 9^{n+1}.$$

Thus, by induction, a_k contains fewer than 9^k fractions for all $k = 1, 2, 3, \ldots$.

As a result, we have $a_n < 9^n/10^{n-1}$. Thus the series in question has a sum which is less than

$$\frac{9}{10^0} + \frac{9^2}{10} + \frac{9^3}{10^2} + \cdots + \frac{9^n}{10^{n-1}} + \cdots = \frac{9}{1 - \frac{9}{10}} = 90.$$

Hence the series converges.

The same proof serves to show that the harmonic series, reduced by striking all fractions containing an 8, or a 7, . . . , or a 1, all converge. A slight adjustment in the proof is required to obtain the result in the case of the digit 0. However, in all cases the series converge. (See Hardy [4].)

Now the number of fractions remaining in a_n above was seen to be less than 9^n, and the total number in all the groups $a_1, a_2, \ldots, a_n$ was less than $9 + 9^2 + \cdots + 9^n = 9(9^n - 1)/(9 - 1)$. These terms encompass all denominators up to, but not including, 10^{n+1}. Of these $10^{n+1} - 1$ denominators, then, the number which were deleted must have been *greater than* $10^{n+1} - 1 - 9(9^n - 1)/(9 - 1)$. That is to say,

$$\frac{\text{the number of natural numbers} < 10^{n+1} \text{ not containing a 9}}{\text{the number of natural numbers} < 10^{n+1} \text{ which do contain a 9}}$$

$$< \frac{\dfrac{9(9^n - 1)}{9 - 1}}{10^{n+1} - 1 - \dfrac{9(9^n - 1)}{9 - 1}} = \frac{9(9^n - 1)}{8(10^{n+1} - 1) - 9(9^n - 1)}$$

$$< \frac{9(9^n)}{8\left[9(\underbrace{11 \ldots 1)}_{\substack{n+1 \\ \text{digits}}}\right] - 9(9^n - 1)} < \frac{9^n}{8(10^n) - (9^n - 1)}$$

$$< \frac{9^n}{8 \cdot 10^n - 9^n} = \frac{1}{8\left(\dfrac{10}{9}\right)^n - 1}.$$

Clearly, as $n \to \infty$, this ratio $\to 0$. Consequently, over a "large" range of natural numbers from 0 to m, "almost all" the numbers contain the digit 9. Over the totality of natural numbers, then, the probability is zero that a number chosen at random will not contain a 9. But the same can be said for every other digit $0, 1, 2, \ldots, 8$. Thus we have the conclusion that it is a probabilistic certainty that a natural number chosen at random contains every digit 0 to 9 at least once. This is not so surprising when you consider that "most" natural numbers contain millions of digits. In normal life we deal with numbers which contain only a few digits and we are sometimes taken aback by the results of large-scale random selections.

2. Partial Sums of the Harmonic Series. The harmonic series, while divergent, grows very slowly. The question of the minimum number of terms required to yield a partial sum which exceeds a specified value has been taken up by several mathematicians. For example, the sum of a quarter of a billion terms is still less than 20. In order to surpass 100, it is necessary to add up more than 15 million trillion trillion trillion terms. (See the paper by Boas and Wrench [3].) A. D. Wadhwa [5] has shown that the sum S of the convergent series obtained by deleting all terms containing the digit 0 is between 20.2 and 28.3. However, almost 60 years ago, Frank Irwin gave the better bounds $22.4 < S < 23.3$, and more recently Ralph Boas has shown that $S = 23.10345$ is correct to five places of decimals.

This topic seems far from exhausted, for there are still many variations to be considered. For example, what kind of series results upon the deletion of all terms containing an odd digit?

Exercises

1. Let S denote the sum of the terms remaining in the harmonic series upon the deletion of all terms whose denominators contain any *even* digit. Prove that $S < 7$.

2. Prove indirectly that the harmonic series diverges by showing that if $S = 1 + \dfrac{1}{2} + \dfrac{1}{3} + \cdots + \dfrac{1}{n} + \cdots$, then $S > S$.

3. If $N = 1 + \dfrac{1}{2} + \dfrac{1}{3} + \cdots + \dfrac{1}{n}$, prove that $e^N > n + 1$.

4. Prove that $1 + \dfrac{1}{2} + \dfrac{1}{3} + \cdots + \dfrac{1}{n}$ is never an integer.

References

1. A. J. Kempner, A curious convergent series, Amer. Math. Monthly, 21 (1914) 48.

2. Frank Irwin, A curious convergent series, Amer. Math. Monthly, 23 (1916) 149.

3. R. P. Boas and J. W. Wrench, Partial sums of the harmonic series, Amer. Math. Monthly, 78 (1971) 864.

4. G. H. Hardy and E. M. Wright, An Introduction To The Theory of Numbers, Oxford, New York, p. 120.

5. A. D. Wadhwa, An interesting subseries of the harmonic series, Amer. Math. Monthly, 82 (1975) 931.

CHAPTER 11

CHVÁTAL'S ART GALLERY THEOREM

At a conference in Stanford in August, 1973, Victor Klee asked the gifted young Czech mathematician Václav Chvátal (University of Montreal) whether he had considered a certain problem of guarding the paintings in an art gallery. The way the rooms in museums and galleries snake around with all kinds of alcoves and corners, it is not an easy job to keep an eye on every bit of wall space. The question is to determine the minimum number of guards that are necessary to survey the entire building. The guards are to remain at fixed posts, but they are able to turn around on the spot. The walls of the gallery are assumed to be straight. In a short time, Chvátal had the whole matter figured out. He showed that if the gallery has n walls (i.e., if the floor-plan is an n-gon), then, whatever its zig-zag shape (Figure 85), the minimum number of guards needed is never more than $[n/3]$ the integer part of $n/3$. His proof is not difficult.

Proof. First of all, the gallery is triangulated by drawing nonintersecting diagonals in its interior. It is not uncommon for several triangles to come together at a vertex, forming a fan. Clearly, a guard posted just inside a fan at its "center" (the vertex at which all the triangles meet) can see all the wall space it contains. Now there are in general many ways of putting the triangles together in fans ($\triangle ABC$ may be considered to be in a fan centered at A, or at B or C). Chvátal shows that whatever particular triangulation is at hand, it can be decomposed into m fans, where m need not exceed $[n/3]$. Thus not more than $[n/3]$ guards are needed. It is evident from Figure 86, however, that some cases require the full $[n/3]$

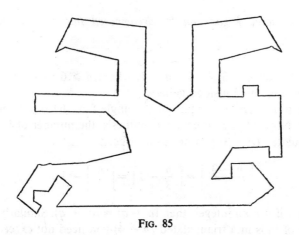

FIG. 85

guards. (There are 3 edges associated with each "peak," and a guard is needed for each peak.) Thus $[n/3]$ is a sharp bound.

The proof that $m \leqslant [n/3]$ is by induction. We observe that if $n = 3, 4,$ or 5, every triangulation is, itself, just a fan (Figure 87). For such n, $[n/3] = 1$, establishing the result for these values.

We take as the induction hypothesis that the statement

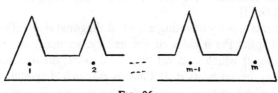

FIG. 86

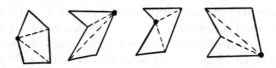

FIG. 87

a triangulated k-gon can be decomposed into m fans, where
$m \leqslant [k/3]$

is valid for all $k = 3, 4, \ldots, n - 1$, where $n \geqslant 6$. Now we consider a triangulated n-sided gallery.

If the triangulation is again just a single fan, the result follows trivially. Now, by the induction hypothesis, the number of fans in a triangulated $(n - 3)$-gon need not exceed

$$\left[\frac{n-3}{3} \right] = \left[\frac{n}{3} - 1 \right] = \left[\frac{n}{3} \right] - 1$$

(note that if q is an integer, then $[a + q] = [a] + q$). Similarly, the number of fans in a triangulated $(n - 4)$-gon need not exceed

$$\left[\frac{n-4}{3} \right] \leqslant \left[\frac{n-3}{3} \right] = \left[\frac{n}{3} \right] - 1.$$

What Chvátal shows is that, in every triangulation, there exists either a triangulated $(n - 3)$-gon or a triangulated $(n - 4)$-gon, with its $[n/3] - 1$ or fewer fans, which gives rise to a fan-decomposition of the whole n-gon which requires not more than 1 additional fan. Thus the total for the n-gon need not exceed the required $[n/3]$.

He proves this by selecting a special diagonal d as follows. Each diagonal splits the n sides of the gallery, so many on each side. Any diagonal which cuts off exactly 4 sides, on one side or the other, may be taken as d. If there is no such diagonal, then any diagonal which cuts off exactly 5 sides will do. If, again, there is no diagonal which does this, any diagonal which cuts off exactly 6 sides is acceptable. So long as there is a diagonal which cuts off more than 3 sides, one must eventually encounter a diagonal with the acceptable minimal property that it cuts off $k \geqslant 4$ sides but no other diagonal cuts off $4, 5, \ldots, k - 1$ sides. But every triangulation contains at least one diagonal which cuts off more than 3 sides. In order to have fewer than 4 sides of the gallery on each side of a diagonal, the total number of sides could not exceed $3 + 3 = 6$. But even in a 6-gon at least 2 of the 3 diagonals in the

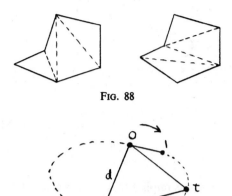

Fig. 88

Fig. 89

triangulation cut off 4 sides. Thus a special d exists in every triangulation (Figure 88).

Now, let the vertices around the gallery be labelled cyclically $0, 1, 2, \ldots, n - 1$, so that the endpoints of d are 0 and k, denoted $d = (0, k)$, as shown in Figure 89. Each diagonal bounds two triangles in a triangulation. Suppose that $(0, t, k)$, where $0 < t < k$, is one of the triangles bounded by d. The side $(0, t)$ cuts t sides from the n-gon. By the distinguishing property of d, no diagonal cuts off $4, 5, \ldots, k - 1$ sides. But $t < k$. Thus it must be that $t \leqslant 3$. Similarly, the side (t, k) cuts off $k - t$ sides, where $k - t < k$. Thus we have also that $k - t \leqslant 3$. Consequently, we obtain the somewhat surprising result that $k \leqslant 3 + t \leqslant 6$. That is to say, there is always some diagonal d which cuts off exactly $4, 5,$ or 6 sides of the gallery.

We observe that d partitions the gallery into a $(k + 1)$-gon and an $(n - k + 1)$-gon. Let G_1 denote the part of the triangulation which is contained in the $(k + 1)$-gon and G_2 the part in the $(n - k + 1)$-gon (Figure 90). Since $k = 4, 5,$ or 6, the $(n - k + 1)$-gon is either an $(n - 3)$, $(n - 4)$, or $(n - 5)$-gon. Observing that

$$\left[\frac{n - 5}{3} \right] \leqslant \left[\frac{n - 4}{3} \right] \leqslant \left[\frac{n - 3}{3} \right] = \left[\frac{n}{3} \right] - 1,$$

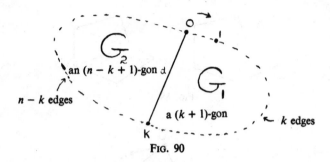

FIG. 90

the induction hypothesis implies that the triangles of G_2 can be put together into m' fans, where $m' \leqslant [n/3] - 1$.

If $k = 4$, the $(k + 1)$-gon G_1 is a 5-gon and its triangulation must be just another fan. Of course, if $k = 5$ or 6, it may also happen that G_1 is a single fan. In such a case, we have the entire n-gon decomposed into $m = m' + 1 \leqslant [n/3]$ fans, as required.

Suppose, then, that G_1 is not a fan. This means $k = 5$ or $k = 6$. Suppose $k = 5$ (Figure 91).

$k = 5$.

In this case, the presence of either of the diagonals $(0, 4)$ or $(1, 5)$ would violate the minimality of k (each of these cuts off only 4 sides). Consequently, the triangle T in G_1 which is bounded by d is either $(0, 2, 5)$ or $(0, 3, 5)$. Since these are equivalent cases, let us suppose, for definiteness, that T is $(0, 2, 5)$. The rest of G_1 is triangle $(0, 1, 2)$ and quadrilateral $(2, 3, 4, 5)$. Either diagonal of a quadrilateral triangulates it. However, the diagonal $(2, 4)$ would

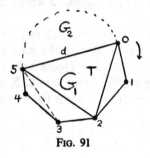

FIG. 91

make G_1 into a single fan (centered at 2). Since this is not the case, it must be triangulated by diagonal (3, 5).

Now consider the $(n - 3)$-gon G_0 which is determined by the union of G_2 and T. By the induction hypothesis, the triangles therein go together into $m' \leqslant [n/3] - 1$ fans. Let F denote the particular fan which contains T. Since F contains T, it must be centered at one of its vertices, 0, 2, or 5. If it is centered at 2, then T would have to be the only triangle in F, and therefore F could be considered to be centered at any of the three vertices. Thus, without loss of generality, F may be taken to be centered at 0 or 5.

If F is centered at 5, it can be extended to include the two triangles of quadrilateral (2, 3, 4, 5). Letting triangle (0, 1, 2) itself comprise an additional fan, we have the whole n-gon covered with $m = m' + 1 \leqslant [n/3]$ fans, as required. If it is centered at 0, we extend it to take in the triangle (0, 1, 2), and add a new fan at 5 to include the two triangles of quadrilateral (2, 3, 4, 5). The conclusion again follows. Finally, suppose $k = 6$.

$k = 6$.

This time the diagonals (0, 5), (0, 4), (1, 6), (2, 6) all violate the minimality of k. Thus T must be the triangle (0, 3, 6). The rest of G_1 is two quadrilaterals. If each of these is triangulated with a diagonal from 3, G_1 would be a single fan. Thus two cases arise, determined by the use of (i) none, or (ii) one of the diagonals from 3.

In case (i), we adjoin T to G_2 to produce an $(n - 4)$-gon G_0. The number of fans m' in G_0 need not exceed $[(n - 4)/3] \leqslant [n/3] - 1$. The fan F which contains T is centered, without loss of generality, at 0 or 6. But these cases are equivalent. Suppose F is centered at 0. Then extend F to include the two triangles of quadrilateral (0, 1, 2, 3) and add a new fan at 6 to pick up the triangles in (3, 4, 5, 6). The desired conclusion follows. (See Figure 92.)

In case (ii), suppose the diagonals are (0, 2) and (3, 5) (the case of (1, 3) and (4, 6) is equivalent). This time we adjoin both T and the triangle M (0, 2, 3) to G_2 to give an $(n - 3)$-gon G_0, with no more than $[n/3] - 1$ fans. Both T and M are contained somewhere in these fans. Consider the fan F which contains M. Without loss of generality, it can be taken to be centered at 0 or 3.

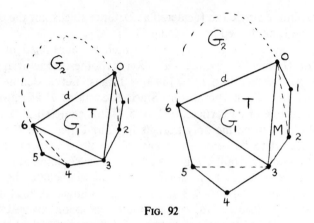

FIG. 92

If it is centered at 0, extend it to include triangle (0, 1, 2) and add a new fan at 3 to include the triangles of (3, 4, 5, 6). If centered at 3, extend it to include T (if it doesn't already) and the triangles in (3, 4, 5, 6) and add a new fan at 0 to get triangle (0, 1, 2). In every case, the entire n-gon is decomposed into not more than $[n/3]$ fans, and the theorem follows.

CHAPTER 12

THE SET OF DISTANCES DETERMINED BY
n POINTS IN THE PLANE

1. A set of *n* points in the plane determines a total of $\binom{n}{2}$ distances. Presumably they might all be the same, or perhaps all different. In fact, however, this is generally far from the truth. For example, among the 91 distances determined by 14 points in the plane there must always occur at least 4 different distances, the greatest distance of the set can never arise more than 14 times, the least distance not more than 36 times, while no distance can occur more often than 40 times. We shall show for *n* points in the plane, $n = 3, 4, 5, \ldots,$ that

- (i) there are at least $\sqrt{n - \frac{3}{4}} - \frac{1}{2}$ different distances,
- (ii) the minimum distance can occur not more than $3n - 6$ times,
- (iii) the maximum distance can occur only *n* times,
- (iv) no distance can occur as often as $\dfrac{n^{3/2}}{\sqrt{2}} + \dfrac{n}{4}$ times.

The proofs are elementary and ingenious and they are taken essentially from the 1946 output of the renowned Paul Erdös [1]. Except for (iii), some of these bounds have been improved and further sharpening would not be surprising. It strikes me as remarkable, however, that such numerical restrictions are inherent in the familiar property of "lying flat in a plane."

2. There Are at Least $\sqrt{n - \frac{3}{4}} - \frac{1}{2}$ Different Distances. At the outset, we are likely to view the points democratically, not seeing one as particularly different from another. However, a useful classification distinguishes the points on the "outside" from the "inner" ones. Imagining a nail at each point, an elastic band enclosing the set contracts to touch some of the points, the outer ones, and misses others on the inside. The polygon determined by the rubber band is called the "convex hull" of the set and is a notion of fundamental importance in investigations of this sort (Figure 93).

Let the points be labelled $P_1, P_2, \ldots, P_n$. We focus our attention on any one of the points, say P_1, which occurs on the convex hull, and we observe that the angle of the hull at the point P_1 does not exceed a straight angle. Consider now just the $n - 1$ distances which emanate from P_1, namely $P_1P_2, P_1P_3, \ldots, P_1P_n$. Suppose that there are k different distances $d_1, d_2, \ldots, d_k$ among these $n - 1$ distances. Suppose also that d_1 occurs among them f_1 times, that d_2 occurs f_2 times, etc. Then, altogether, the number of distances in this subset is

$$f_1 + f_2 + \cdots + f_k = n - 1.$$

Let the maximum value among the frequencies f_i be denoted N. Then

$$f_1 + f_2 + \cdots + f_k$$

$$\leqslant N + N + \cdots + N = kN.$$

Hence $n - 1 \leqslant Nk$, and we obtain $k \geqslant (n - 1)/N$.

Next, let r denote a distance, among the $n - 1$ under investigation, which occurs with the maximum frequency N. The circle $P_1(r)$ (i.e., with center P_1 and radius r) then passes through N of the points of the given set, say $Q_1, Q_2, \ldots, Q_N$ (Figure 94). Because the angle of the convex hull at P_1 does not exceed a straight angle, these N points Q_i are confined to a semicircle of $P_1(r)$. Therefore the $N - 1$ distances $Q_1Q_2, Q_1Q_3, \ldots, Q_1Q_N$ are all different. Thus we have identified two subsets of distances

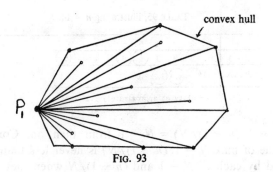

FIG. 93

which contain, respectively, at least $N - 1$ and $k \geqslant (n - 1)/N$ different distances. New distances elsewhere in the set only increase the count. Hence the number of different distances in the entire set cannot be less than the greater of the two numbers $N - 1$ and $(n - 1)/N$, which is denoted $\max(N - 1, (n - 1)/N)$. It remains only to observe that $\max(N - 1, (n - 1)/N)$ is never less than $\sqrt{n - \frac{3}{4}} - \frac{1}{2}$.

Considering, in order, the various possibilities $N = 1, N = 2, \ldots, N = n - 1$ (see Table 95, illustrating the case $n = 14$), we see that $N - 1$ is smaller than $(n - 1)/N$ at the start, making $\max(N - 1, (n - 1)/N) = (n - 1)/N$ in the early cases, but that the increasing $N - 1$ catches up to the decreasing $(n - 1)/N$, and

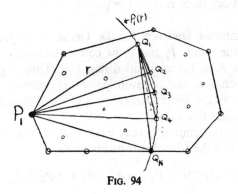

FIG. 94

TABLE 95, illustrating $n = 14$.

N	1	2	3	4	5	6	.	.	.	13	max ($N-1$, $\frac{n-1}{N}$)
$N-1$	0	1	2	3	④	⑤	.	.	.	⑬	is circled
$\frac{n-1}{N}$	⑬	⑥.5	④.3	③.2	2.6	2.2	.	.	.	1	

equality at approximately 3.14

$\max(N-1, (n-1)/N) = N-1$ from then on. Consequently the value of $\max(N-1, (n-1)/N)$ is never less than the value attained by each of $N-1$ and $(n-1)/N$ when they are equal. This occurs for

$$N - 1 = \frac{n-1}{N},$$

$$N^2 - N - (n-1) = 0,$$

$$N = \frac{1 \pm \sqrt{1 + 4(n-1)}}{2}$$

$$= \frac{1 \pm \sqrt{4n-3}}{2} = \frac{1}{2} \pm \sqrt{n - \tfrac{3}{4}} \ .$$

Since N is at least 1, we have $N = \frac{1}{2} + \sqrt{n - \tfrac{3}{4}}$. The common value in question, then, is $N - 1 = \sqrt{n - \tfrac{3}{4}} - \frac{1}{2}$.

3. The Minimum Distance Cannot Occur More than $3n - 6$ Times. Let the points P_i and P_j be connected with a segment if and only if P_iP_j is the minimal distance r'. Thus a graph G is obtained which has the n given points as vertices and some segments r' as edges. First we show that G is a planar graph, that is, it has no edges that cross.

Suppose, to the contrary, that edge P_1P_2 crosses P_3P_4 at O (Figure 96). Then the triangle inequality gives

$$OP_1 + OP_3 > P_1P_3 \quad \text{and} \quad OP_2 + OP_4 > P_2P_4.$$

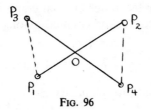

FIG. 96

Adding yields $P_1P_2 + P_3P_4 > P_1P_3 + P_2P_4$, which is $2r'$ $> P_1P_3 + P_2P_4$. Consequently, not both P_1P_3 and P_2P_4 can be as great as r', a contradiction. Thus G is a planar graph.

Now G may be disconnected and have edges scattered about so that they fail to join with others to bound a face. This makes it awkward to see how the famous Euler formula $V - E + F = 2$ applies. It is assumed that the reader's background contains the application of Euler's formula to a single component (i.e., connected piece) of a planar graph. Suppose that our graph is in c pieces. Then $c - 1$ extra edges may be used to string the components together into a connected whole G' (Figure 97). None of these extra (connecting) edges can bound a face. Thus we still have the same number of faces, and Euler's formula applied to G' yields

$$V - (E + c - 1) + F = 2,$$

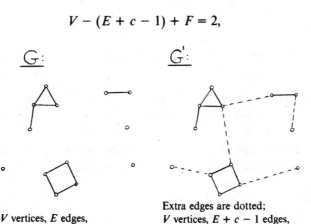

V vertices, E edges, F faces, c components

Extra edges are dotted; V vertices, $E + c - 1$ edges, F faces, 1 component.

FIG. 97

where V, E, and F refer to our original graph G. (We should note that the infinite outer face is counted among the F faces of G.) Thus we have

$$E = V + F - c - 1.$$

Since $c \geqslant 1$, we obtain the inequality

$$E \leqslant V + F - 2,$$

connecting just the parameters of the original graph G.

Since it takes at least 3 edges to enclose a face, the F faces of G must account for at least $3F$ edges altogether. Because an edge may bound no more than 2 faces (some edges may bound only one or none at all), this total of $3F$ cannot amount to more than $2E$ (which would allow for every edge to be involved twice). Thus we have

$$3F \leqslant 2E, \quad \text{and} \quad F \leqslant \tfrac{2}{3}E.$$

Accordingly, we have

$$E \leqslant V + F - 2 \leqslant V + \tfrac{2}{3}E - 2,$$

giving

$$\frac{E}{3} \leqslant V - 2, \quad \text{and} \quad E \leqslant 3V - 6.$$

But V is simply n, and we obtain $E \leqslant 3n - 6$. Thus the number of minimal distances r' cannot exceed $3n - 6$.

4. The Maximum Distance Can Occur only n Times. We proceed by induction. Clearly our claim holds for $n = 3$, since, in this case, there are only 3 distances altogether. Suppose, then, for any set of $n - 1$ points, the maximum distance can occur not more than $n - 1$ times. Suppose also that some set S, with n points, violates our condition by possessing more than n maximal segments r. We argue now to a contradiction.

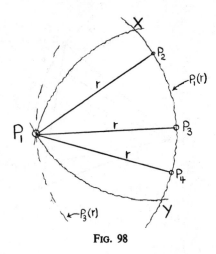

Fig. 98

The number of endpoints belonging to these maximal segments must therefore exceed $2n$, implying that the average number of endpoints per given point of S exceeds $2\ (= 2n/n)$. Accordingly, some point P_1 of S must have (at least) three maximal segments P_1P_2, P_1P_3, P_1P_4 emanating from it (Figure 98). Since no two of P_2, P_3, P_4 can determine a distance exceeding r, the three points are confined to a $60°$ arc of the circle $P_1(r)$. In this arc, let P_3 lie between P_2 and P_4.

Now every circle $P_i(r)$ must enclose the entire set S, lest some P_iP_j exceed the maximum r. Thus S is bounded by the intersection P_1XY of the three circles $P_1(r)$, $P_2(r)$, and $P_4(r)$. (If $\angle P_2P_1P_4 = 60°$, then X coincides with P_2 and Y with P_4.) Because P_3 is between P_2 and P_4, the circumference of $P_3(r)$ makes contact with this region P_1XY only at the point P_1. Consequently, the only point of S which is at a distance r from P_3 is the point P_1. Hence, from P_3 there emanates only one maximal segment r.

Deleting P_3 from S leaves a set of $n-1$ points with one less maximal segment. Since there were more than n such segments to begin with, there still must remain more than $n-1$ of them. But this contradicts the induction hypothesis, and the conclusion follows.

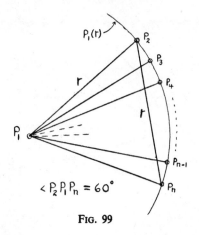

FIG. 99

We observe that, for every n, there does exist a set possessing n maximal distances. Thus we may sharpen our conclusion: the maximum distance can occur only n times (Figure 99).

5. No Distance Can Occur as Often as $n^{3/2}/\sqrt{2} + (n/4)$ Times. In 1946 Paul Erdös gave a very clever proof that no distance can occur as often as $n^{3/2}$ times. This gem is given in the Appendix. Here we prove the better result that no distance can occur even $n^{3/2}/\sqrt{2} + (n/4)$ times.

Let r denote any distance which occurs in the set and let X denote the number of times it occurs. Let the points P_i and P_j be joined by a segment if and only if $P_iP_j = r$. Suppose that x_1 of these joins emanate from P_1, x_2 from P_2, etc. Then x_i counts the number of endpoints which occur at P_i, and the total number altogether is

$$\sum_{i=1}^{n} x_i = 2X, \quad \text{giving } X = \frac{1}{2} \sum_{i=1}^{n} x_i.$$

Now we count the number of paths of length 2 (i.e., pairs of adjacent segments, $P_j \!\circ\!\!-\!\!-\!\!\overset{\displaystyle P_i}{\circ}\!\!-\!\!-\!\!\circ P_k$) which are determined by the segments. Each such path has a "middle" vertex and, since x_i

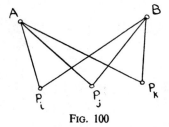

FIG. 100

segments emanate from P_i, the number of these paths which have P_i as middle vertex is $\binom{x_i}{2}$. The total number of these paths, then, is

$$\sum_{i=1}^{n} \binom{x_i}{2}.$$

A path of length 2 connects a pair of "outer" vertices. The n given points provide a total of $\binom{n}{2}$ pairs for these extremities. Consequently, if the number of paths of length 2 exceeds twice the number of pairs (i.e., $2\binom{n}{2}$), the Dirichlet pigeon-hole principle implies that some pair of vertices A and B must serve as the extremities of (at least) three paths (Figure 100). But, because all the segments are the same length r, this demands the impossible requirement that two different circles, $A(r)$ and $B(r)$, intersect in three points. Thus the number of paths of length 2 cannot exceed $2\binom{n}{2}$; i.e.,

$$\sum_{i=1}^{n} \binom{x_i}{2} \leqslant n(n-1). \tag{1}$$

Expanding the left side of this relation, we get

$$\sum_{i=1}^{n} \binom{x_i}{2} = \sum_{i=1}^{n} \frac{x_i(x_i-1)}{2} = \frac{1}{2}\sum_{i=1}^{n} x_i^2 - \frac{1}{2}\sum_{i=1}^{n} x_i,$$

or

$$\sum_{i=1}^{n} \binom{x_i}{2} = \frac{1}{2} \sum_{i=1}^{n} x_i^2 - X. \tag{2}$$

But it is easy to see that $\sum_{i=1}^{n} x_i^2 \geq 4X^2/n$. To this end, we note that

$$(x_1 + x_2 + \cdots + x_n)^2 = \left(\sum_{i=1}^{n} x_i \right)^2$$

$$= \sum_{i=1}^{n} x_i^2 + 2 \sum_{\substack{i,j=1 \\ i \neq j}}^{n} x_i x_j,$$

and that

$$\sum_{\substack{i,j=1 \\ i \neq j}}^{n} (x_i - x_j)^2 = (n-1) \sum_{i=1}^{n} x_i^2 - 2 \sum_{\substack{i,j=1 \\ i \neq j}}^{n} x_i x_j.$$

Adding clears away the "cross-products," giving simply

$$\left(\sum_{i=1}^{n} x_i \right)^2 + \sum_{i,j=1 \, i \neq j}^{n} (x_i - x_j)^2 = n \sum_{i=1}^{n} x_i^2.$$

Since $(x_i - x_j)^2 \geq 0$, we obtain $(\sum_{i=1}^{n} x_i)^2 \leq n \sum_{i=1}^{n} x_i^2$, or

$$\sum_{i=1}^{n} x_i^2 > \frac{1}{n} (2X)^2 = \frac{4X^2}{n}.$$

as promised.

Substituting in (2), we have

$$\sum_{i=1}^{n} \binom{x_i}{2} > \frac{2X^2}{n} - X.$$

Combining with (1), then, we obtain

$$\frac{2X^2}{n} - X \leqslant n(n-1), \quad 2X^2 - nX - n^2(n-1) \leqslant 0.$$

This quadratic function (Figure 101) takes nonpositive values for X in the closed interval between the roots of the corresponding equation, restricting X to the range

$$\frac{n}{4}(1 - \sqrt{8n-7}) \leqslant X \leqslant \frac{n}{4}(1 + \sqrt{8n-7}).$$

Thus the distance r cannot occur more often than $(n/4)(1 + \sqrt{8n-7})$ times. And this is smaller than the stated $(n/4)(1 + \sqrt{8n}) = (n/4) + n^{3/2}/\sqrt{2}$.

As a corollary, we obtain the result that the $\binom{n}{2}$ distances determined by the n points must give rise to more than

$$\frac{\binom{n}{2}}{\dfrac{n}{4} + \dfrac{n^{3/2}}{\sqrt{2}}}$$

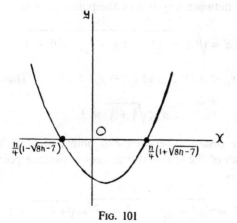

FIG. 101

different distances. The order of magnitude of this result is $n^{1/2}$, but it is not as good a bound as the earlier $\sqrt{n - \frac{3}{4}} - \frac{1}{2}$.

6. Additional Results.

(a) We have seen that the maximum distance determined by n points in the plane can occur only n times. In 3-dimensional space, it has been shown that it can occur not more than $2n - 2$ times [2]. In 1955, Lenz discovered that, in 4-dimensional space, the maximum distance can occur as often as $[n^2/4]$ (the integer part of $n^2/4$). He simply constructed a set with this property as follows:

There are any number of pairs (x, y), with $0 < x, y < 1/\sqrt{2}$, such that $x^2 + y^2 = \frac{1}{2}$ (i.e., the circle $x^2 + y^2 = \frac{1}{2}$ has infinitely many points in the first quadrant). Choose any n such pairs, $(x_1, y_1), (x_2, y_2), (x_3, y_3), \ldots, (x_n, y_n)$. Let $[n/2] = s$, and use the first s of these pairs to determine the set A of 4-dimensional points

$$A: \quad (x_1, y_1, 0, 0), (x_2, y_2, 0, 0), \ldots, (x_s, y_s, 0, 0),$$

and use the remaining $n - s$ pairs to determine the set B

$$B: \quad (0, 0, x_{s+1}, y_{s+1}), (0, 0, x_{s+2}, y_{s+2}), \ldots, (0, 0, x_n, y_n).$$

The distance between any two of the points in A is

$$d = \sqrt{(x_i - x_j)^2 + (y_i - y_j)^2 + 0 + 0},$$

where $|x_i - x_j| < 1/\sqrt{2}$ and $|y_i - y_j| < 1/\sqrt{2}$. Thus

$$d < \sqrt{\tfrac{1}{2} + \tfrac{1}{2}} = 1.$$

Similarly, the distance between two points of B is less than 1. However, each of the $s(n - s)$ distances between a point of A and a point of B is

$$d' = \sqrt{x_i^2 + y_i^2 + x_j^2 + y_j^2} = \sqrt{\tfrac{1}{2} + \tfrac{1}{2}} = 1.$$

Thus 1 is the maximum distance determined by the set $A \cup B$. And it occurs $s(n - s)$ times. It remains only to note that $s(n - s) = [n^2/4]$.

If n is even, say $2k$, then $s = [n/2] = [k] = k$, and $s(n - s) = k(2k - k) = k^2$, while $[n^2/4] = [4k^2/4] = [k^2] = k^2$. If n is odd, say $2k + 1$, then $s = [n/2] = [k + \frac{1}{2}] = k$, and $s(n - s) = k(2k + 1 - k) = k(k + 1) = k^2 + k$, while $[n^2/4] = [(4k^2 + 4k + 1)/4] = [k^2 + k + \frac{1}{4}] = k^2 + k$.

(b) There exists a fixed number c such that, for all n, no distance determined by a set of n points in 3-dimensional space occurs more than $cn^{5/3}$ times [3].

(c) The five vertices of a regular pentagon and its circumcenter provide a set of 6 points in the plane with the property that every 3 of the points determine an *isosceles* triangle (Figure 102).

In 3-dimensional space this same configuration leads to a set of 8 points all of whose $\binom{8}{3} = 56$ triangles are isosceles. One simply adds the point P on the line through the circumcenter, perpendicular to the plane of the pentagon, at a distance from it equal to the circumradius, and also the mirror image of P on the other side of the plane.

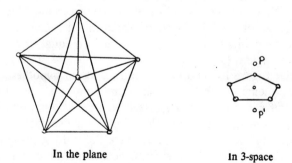

In the plane   In 3-space

FIG. 102

We conclude our story with a proof of the fact that no set of n points in the plane, which has more than 6 points, can be an isosceles n-point, i.e., determine only isosceles triangles. This was posed by Erdös as a problem in the American Mathematical Monthly (1946, Volume 53, page 394). We follow the nicely organized solution of L. M. Kelly (1947, Volume 54, pages 227–229). This assures us that, for $n = 7$, at least 3 different distances must occur. Our earlier result promises only $\sqrt{7 - \frac{3}{4}} - \frac{1}{2} = 2$ (exactly).

Kelly's long proof is in 7 parts. Nevertheless, we give the entire development in detail because most of the parts contain very nice arguments. His attack is as follows. First he deduces that a certain 4-point configuration F must be contained in every isosceles 6-point. Clearly, no k-point subset of an isosceles n-point can, itself, fail to be an isosceles k-point. Starting out with an isosceles 4-point F, he builds up the set by adding points at places which continue to keep all triangles isosceles. It turns out that the fifth point can be added only at one of two places. Thus eliminating all the other points of the plane except two, we achieve an extension to the isosceles 5-point and we see that 6 is an upper bound on the number of points possible in an isosceles n-point. The realization of the isosceles 6-point, as described above, then, establishes 6 as the maximum, and the conclusion follows.

(i) **The Configuration F.** Let 1, 2, 3, 4, 5, 6 denote the points of an isosceles 6-point. We establish that for some point of the set there must be at least three others which are the same distance away. Let the points be joined in pairs. Let two equal sides of the isosceles triangle 123 be $12 = 13 = a$, and let $14 = x$, $15 = y$, $16 = z$. (See Figure 103.) Suppose, contrary to our hypothesis, that no three segments radiating from the same point are equal. In this case, none of x, y, z can equal a, lest three a's run from point 1.

Now we know that each triangle is isosceles. Therefore a triangle with unequal sides p and q must have the third side duplicate either p or q. In $\triangle 142$, then, 24 must be either a or x (which are different), and similarly for 34 in $\triangle 143$. However, both 24 and 34 cannot be x, lest three x's radiate from 4. Thus one of them must

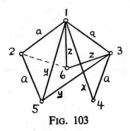

FIG. 103

be *a*, say 34 (the cases are equivalent). This gives two segments *a* from 3 (31 and 34). Thus 35 cannot also be *a*. From △351, then, we see that 35 must be *y*. Similarly, 36, in △136, must be *z*. Also, 25 in △125 must be *a*, lest three *y*'s emanate from 5. Finally, in △126, 26 must be *a* or *z*. Consequently, we have either three *a*'s from 2, or three *z*'s from 6. This contradiction establishes the necessity of every isosceles 6-point containing a point *P* from which three equal segments *PQ*, *PR*, *PS* radiate. The triangle *QRS* is isosceles and the point *P* is its circumcenter. Thus the aforementioned configuration *F* is an isosceles triangle with its circumcenter.

(ii) This section is the first of five, in each of which it is shown that a particular configuration cannot possibly occur as part of an isosceles 6-point. The configuration of this section is "a set of three collinear points." Throughout, we continue with the notation 1, 2, 3, 4, 5, 6 for the points of an isosceles 6-point.

Suppose some isosceles 6-point does contain three collinear points 1, 2, 3. Triangle 123, although collapsed, would still have to have two equal distances among its three sides 12, 13, and 23. Let 2 occur between 1 and 3, implying 12 = 23 = *a*, say (Figure 104). Consider now the triangles 124 and 234. Suppose that 24 = *b*, and

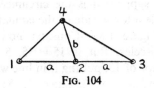

FIG. 104

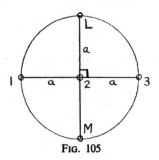

FIG. 105

that it is different from a. Then the equal base angles of $\triangle 124$ are either the pair at 1 and 2 (if $14 = b$), or the pair at 2 and 4 (if $14 = a$). In either case, the angle at 2, namely $\angle 124$, is one of these base angles and, as such, it is acute. Similarly, $\angle 423$ in $\triangle 234$ is also acute, and the sum $\angle 124 + \angle 423$ falls short of a straight angle. This contradiction establishes that $24 = a$.

In this case, 2 is the circumcenter of $\triangle 134$ and 13 is a diameter (Figure 105). Thus $\triangle 134$ is not only isosceles, but right-angled at 4. This makes $14 = 34$, and 42 is perpendicular to 123. Therefore 4 must occur at an end, L or M, of a diameter which is perpendicular to 13 in the circle on 13 as diameter. But 4 is not special. The same argument places 5 and 6 also at these points L and M. Thus two of 4, 5, 6 must coincide, which is impossible. Equivalently, we might have argued that there exist places for only two points in addition to 1, 2, 3, imposing a limit of 5 points on such an isosceles n-point. Thus no isosceles 6-point contains three collinear points.

(iii) We have seen that an isosceles 6-point necessarily contains an isosceles triangle QRS with its circumcenter P. Now we show that the isosceles triangle (QRS) of a configuration F cannot be so thoroughly isosceles as to be equilateral.

To the contrary, suppose 4 is the circumcenter of equilateral triangle 123. Let a denote the side of the equilateral triangle and b its circumradius (Figure 106). Consider now a fifth point, 5. Triangle 135 is isosceles. But if $15 = 35$, 5 would lie on the perpendicular bisector of 13, putting it in line with 2 and 4. This is impossible by (ii), and so in $\triangle 135$ one of 15, 35 must duplicate the

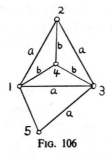

FIG. 106

third side $13 = a$. Suppose, for definiteness, that $35 = a$ and $15 \neq a$.

Now the same argument applied to $\triangle 125$ yields one of 15, 25 equal to a. Since $15 \neq a$, it must be $25 = a$. But then $25 = 35$, and 1, 4, 5 colline. Thus we have a contradiction and the conclusion follows.

(iv) This time we find that a pair of equilateral triangles with a common side is a forbidden configuration. Again, we proceed indirectly. Suppose 123 and 134 are equilateral triangles of side a, and that $24 = b$. Then $b > a$. Consider a point 5 (Figure 107).

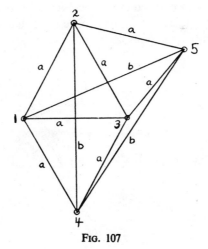

FIG. 107

If 15 = 35, then 5 collines with 2 and 4. Thus, in △135, one and only one of 15, 35 must equal a. The cases are equivalent, so let 35 = a and 15 ≠ a. Similarly, from △245, one of 25, 45 equals b, say 45 = b and 25 ≠ b.

Now, in △145, we have 14 = a and 45 = b. Hence 15 = a or b. But we already have 15 ≠ a. Thus 15 = b. Then, in △125, we have 25 = a or b. We have 25 ≠ b, above, giving 25 = a. This makes △235 equilateral, and ∠435 is a straight angle (being the sum of three angles in equilateral triangles). Thus 4, 3, and 5 are in a straight line, which is impossible.

(v) Let 123 denote an equilateral triangle of side a, and let LM be the diameter of the circle 3(a) which bisects ∠132 (Figure 108). Our final two forbidden configurations consist of the 4-point figures 1234 obtained by putting 4 at L and M. First we consider 4 at L. Let 14 = 24 = b. Then clearly $b < a$.

As we have argued before, 15 ≠ 25, lest 3, 4, 5 colline. Thus, in △125, one of 15, 25 equals a. Suppose, for definiteness, that 25 = a. Now, in △245, 45 = a or b. Suppose, if possible, that 45 = a. Then, because 25 = 45 = a, and 5 cannot coincide with 3, it must be that 5 is the mirror image of 3 in 24. This makes the angles 542, 243, 341 equal. And it is easy to compute that their measure is 75°. Thus ∠541 must be 135°. In isosceles △145, then, this 135° angle can only be the vertical angle (it is too large for a base angle). This forces 45 and 41 to be the equal arms, implying $a = b$, a contradiction. Thus 45 = b.

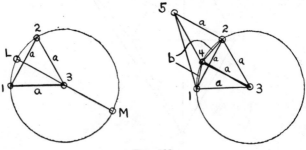

Fig. 108

In △345, then, we have $45 = b$, $34 = a$, and 35 forced to duplicate one of them. But $35 = a$ gives an immediate contradiction: △235 would be equilateral, which either places 5 at 1 or gives a pair of equilateral triangles (123, 235) like the ones just eliminated in the previous section. Therefore $35 = b$, and since $b < a$, this puts 5 inside circle 3(a). (See Figure 109.)

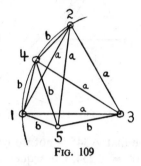

Fig. 109

Now in △125, $12 = 25 = a$. Thus, if also $15 = a$, the triangle is equilateral, forcing 5, which is inside the circle, to occur at the center 3 (impossible). But, from △135, 15 is either a or b. Hence, $15 = b$. Accordingly, $51 = 54 = 53 = b$, making 5 the circumcenter of △143. But the circumcenter of an isosceles triangle lies inside the triangle if the vertical angle is acute ($\angle$ 134 is only 30°). Thus 5 must be inside △143. But $25 = a$, and there is no point inside △143 which is a distance a from 2. Thus 4 cannot go at L.

(vi) Suppose 4 is at M. Here we have $24 = b > a$ (Figure 110).

As in the previous argument, we have $15 \neq 25$, lest 3, 4, 5 colline; from △125, however, one of 15, 25 is a; again, suppose that $25 = a$, and that $15 \neq a$. Now, if $35 = a$, then △235 is equilateral, and to avoid 5 at 1 we obtain the forbidden configuration of two equilateral triangles (123 and 235) with a common base (23). Thus $35 \neq a$. Combining this with $15 \neq a$, we see that the equal sides in △135 must be 15 and 35. Consequently, 5 lies on the perpendicular bisector of 13. Since $25 = a$, 5 occurs on the circle 2(a). Thus 5 must be either at L' or M' in the diagram. However, with 5 at L', we have the forbidden configuration of the previous section in 1, 2, 3, 5. Thus 5 must go at M'.

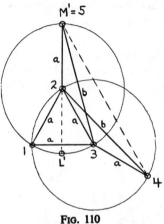

FIG. 110

Now it is easy to see that △345 is not isosceles. Simple calculations give ∠523 = 150° = ∠234. Consequently, the triangles 523 and 234 are congruent, making 35 = 24 = *b*. Also, we easily get ∠532 = 15°, implying ∠534 = 135°. In isosceles △534, then, the equal sides must be 53 and 34 (135° is too much for a base angle), implying *b* = *a*, a contradiction. Thus 4 cannot go at *M*.

(vii) We know that every isosceles 6-point contains a configuration *F*. Now we investigate how such a figure might be extended into an isosceles 5-point. Accordingly, let 1, 2, 3, 4 comprise an *F* with dimensions given by 12 = 13 = 14 = *a*, 24 = 34 = *b*, and 23 = *c*. First we show that no two of *a*, *b*, *c* are equal. (See Figure 111.)

If *a* = *b*, then triangles 124 and 134 would constitute a pair of equilateral triangles on base 14, which is the forbidden configura-

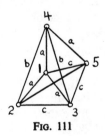

FIG. 111

tion (iv). If $a = c$, then 1, 2, 3, 4 would yield an unacceptable figure of section (v) or (vi). If $b = c$, F would be an equilateral triangle with its circumcenter, which was outlawed in section (iii).

Now we try to place a fifth point 5. If $25 = 35$, then 5 collines with 1 and 4. Thus $25 \neq 35$, and in $\triangle 235$ we have one of 25, 35 equal c. The cases are equivalent, so let $35 = c$.

Next we determine 15. From $\triangle 135$, it is either a or c. Suppose $15 = c$, as illustrated. In $\triangle 125$, 25 must duplicate a or c. But, as seen above, $25 \neq 35 = c$. Thus $25 = a$. Now from $\triangle 145$, 45 is either a or c, and from $\triangle 245$, 45 is either a or b. Thus 45 must be a. In this case, $\triangle 345$ has sides a, b, and c, and fails to be isosceles. Thus $15 = a$.

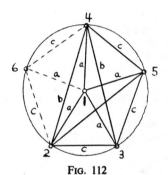

FIG. 112

Combining this with $35 = c$, we see that the position of 5 is already completely nailed down (Figure 112). The point 2 is one of the points of intersection of the circles $1(a)$ and $3(c)$ and 5 is the other. The equivalent case of $25 = c$ (we supposed $35 = c$) similarly places 5 at the second intersection 6 of the circles $1(a)$ and $2(c)$ (3 is one intersection). Consequently, there exist only two acceptable positions for 5 and, as explained above, our proof is complete.

We are now in a position to see easily that the isosceles 6-point is unique. Because $15 = a$, 1 lies on the perpendicular bisector of 25, as does 3. If $45 = b$, then 4, 1, 3 would colline. Hence $45 \neq b$. In $\triangle 345$, therefore, we must have $45 = c$. The equivalent case of $25 = c$ similarly yields $46 = c$. Thus we see that 45326 has five sides equal to c, and is inscribed in $1(a)$. Thus the isosceles 6-point is uniquely the vertices of a regular pentagon with its center.

Exercise

1. It is known that n points in the plane, not all collinear, determine a line (by joining the points in pairs) which contains only two of the n points [4]. Use this to determine that n points in the plane, not all collinear, determine at least n different lines when joined in pairs.

References

0. Nearly 100 of Erdös' 600 papers are reprinted in the monumental Paul Erdös: The Art of Counting, MIT Press, 1973.

1. Paul Erdös, On the set of distances of n points, Amer. Math. Monthly, 53 (1946) 248–250; also given in **0**.

2. B. Grünbaum, A proof of Vazsonyi's conjecture, Bull. Research Council of Israel, 6A (1956) 77–78.

3. Paul Erdös, On sets of distances of n points in Euclidean space, Magyar Tud. Akad. Mat. Kut. Int. Kozl., 5 (1960) 165–169.

4. Ross Honsberger, Ingenuity in Mathematics, New Mathematical Library, vol. 23, Mathematical Association of America, 1970, 13–16.

APPENDIX

No Distance Can Occur as Often as $n^{3/2}$ Times.

We use the same notation as in the essay: the distance r occurs X times altogether, x_1 times at P_1, x_2 times at P_2, etc.; then $X = \frac{1}{2}\sum_{i=1}^{n} x_i$. Suppose also that the points have been examined in advance and the labels assigned so that

$$x_1 \geqslant x_2 \geqslant x_3 \geqslant \cdots \geqslant x_n.$$

Now it may not happen that all n of the points are endpoints of distances r. (Since $X \geqslant 1$, the two greatest x_i, namely x_1 and x_2, must be at least 1, but it is possible for other x_i to be zero.) We

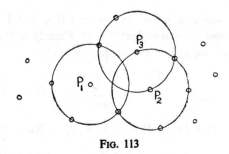

FIG. 113

propose to gather up the points which are the endpoints of distances r by considering, in turn, the circles $P_1(r), P_2(r), \ldots, P_n(r)$. Clearly, on the circle $P_i(r)$ there occur x_i of these points. Let Z denote the number of such points altogether.

On $P_1(r)$, then, we find $x_1 \geqslant 1$ of the points in question. Thus $Z \geqslant x_1$. And on $P_2(r)$, there are x_2 of these points. However, these circles may intersect (Figure 113). Therefore as many as 2 of these x_2 points on $P_2(r)$ may have been counted already among the points of $P_1(r)$. The number of different points on the two circles $P_1(r)$ and $P_2(r)$ is at least $x_1 + (x_2 - 2)$. Thus we have $Z \geqslant x_1 + (x_2 - 2)$. Again, there are x_3 of our points on $P_3(r)$. But as many as $2 \cdot 2 = 4$ may have been counted earlier on the previous circles. It will be safe to increase our subtotal by $x_3 - 4$, giving a running total of $x_1 + (x_2 - 2) + (x_3 - 4)$. Going from circle to circle, we obtain a sequence of subtotals, each of which errs on the small side, if at all. Thus we have

$$x_1 + (x_2 - 2) + (x_3 - 4) + \cdots + \left[x_i - 2(i - 1) \right] \leqslant Z$$

for all $i = 1, 2, \ldots, n$. But $Z \leqslant n$, the total number of points in the given set. Hence

$$\sum_{k=1}^{i} \left[x_k - 2(k - 1) \right] \leqslant n \quad \text{for } i = 1, 2, \ldots, n.$$

Now the number $n^{1/2}$ may not be a whole number. Let "a" denote the integral part of $n^{1/2}$ and f its fractional part. Then

$n^{1/2} = a + f$, where a is an integer and $0 \leqslant f < 1$. This gives $a = n^{1/2} - f$, and $a^2 = n - 2fn^{1/2} + f^2$. Clearly $0 < a < n$, and for $i = a$, above, we obtain the inequality

$$\sum_{k=1}^{a} \left[x_k - 2(k-1) \right] \leqslant n,$$

$$x_1 + (x_2 - 2) + (x_3 - 4) + \cdots + \left[x_a - 2(a-1) \right] \leqslant n,$$

$$x_1 + x_2 + \cdots + x_a - 2\left[1 + 2 + \cdots + (a-1) \right] \leqslant n,$$

$$x_1 + x_2 + \cdots + x_a - (a-1)a \leqslant n,$$

giving

$$x_1 + x_2 + \cdots + x_a \leqslant n + a^2 - a$$

$$= n + n - 2fn^{1/2} + f^2 - n^{1/2} + f$$

$$= 2n - 2fn^{1/2} + (f^2 - n^{1/2} + f).$$

Since $0 \leqslant f < 1$, also $0 \leqslant f^2 < 1$. Except for the known case $n = 3$, we have $n^{1/2} \geqslant 2$, implying $f^2 - n^{1/2} + f$ is negative. Thus we have

$$x_1 + x_2 + \cdots + x_a < 2n - 2fn^{1/2}$$

$$= 2n^{1/2}(n^{1/2} - f),$$

or

$$x_1 + x_2 + \cdots + x_a < 2n^{1/2}a.$$

Because $x_1 \geqslant x_2 \geqslant \cdots \geqslant x_n$, we have

$$x_1 + x_2 + \cdots + x_a \geqslant x_a + x_a + \cdots + x_a = ax_a.$$

Therefore

$$ax_a < 2n^{1/2}a, \quad \text{and} \quad x_a < 2n^{1/2}.$$

Again, because $x_a \geqslant x_{a+1} \geqslant \cdots \geqslant x_n$, we get

$$x_{a+1} + x_{a+2} + \cdots + x_n \leqslant (n-a)x_a,$$

i.e.,

$$x_{a+1} + x_{a+2} + \cdots + x_n < (n-a)2n^{1/2}.$$

Finally, then,

$$\sum_{i=1}^{n} x_i = (x_1 + x_2 + \cdots + x_a) + (x_{a+1} + \cdots + x_n)$$

$$< 2n^{1/2}a + (n-a)2n^{1/2}$$

$$= 2n^{1/2} \cdot n$$

$$= 2n^{3/2}.$$

Thus

$$X = \frac{1}{2} \sum_{i=1}^{n} x_i < n^{3/2}.$$

CHAPTER 13

A PUTNAM PAPER PROBLEM

The Putnam examination is an annual competition open to mathematics undergraduates in North American universities. The problems posed are very challenging and often require considerable ingenuity. In this essay we take up two solutions to the interesting fifth problem of the 1971 competition.

In a game, one scores on a turn either a points or b points, a and b positive integers with $b < a$. Given that there are 35 nonattainable cumulative scores, and that one of them is 58, what are the values of a and b?

Cumulative scores have the form $ax + by$, x and y nonnegative integers, obtained from scoring a on x turns and b on y turns. Now, if a and b are both divisible by an integer d, then every cumulative score is a multiple of d. For $d > 1$, the multiples of d miss taking the values of an infinity of natural numbers. Thus, if any $d > 1$ divides both a and b, there would be an infinity of unattainable scores, not just 35 of them. Consequently, a and b must be relatively prime numbers.

SOLUTION 1.

Because of certain congruence relations, a table of columns of the residue classes (mod a) displays the nonattainable cumulative scores in simple relief from the infinity of attainable scores. The key lies in the first a multiples of b: $0, b, 2b, \ldots, (a - 1)b$. Since a and b are relatively prime, it turns out that these multiples occur one in each of the columns of residue classes. Clearly every multiple mb is an attainable score (m scores of b and none of a).

TABLE 114

{ scores above are unattainable,
  scores below are attainable

0	1	2	3	4	5	6	7	8	9	10	11	12
13	14	15	16	17	18	19	20	21	22	23	24	25
26	27	28	29	30	31	32	33	34	35	36	37	38
39	40	41	42	43	44	45	46	47	48	49	50	51
52	53	54	55	56	57	58	59	60	61	62	63	64
65	66	67	68	69	70	71	72	73	74	75	76	77
78	79	80	81	82	83	-	-	-	-	-	-	-
-	-	-	-	-	-	-	-	-	-	-	-	-

Remarkably, however, in each column, all the numbers below the aforesaid multiple are attainable while none of the numbers above it are. Table 114 illustrates the case for $a = 13$, $b = 5$; the key multiples are 0, 5, 10, 15, ..., 55, 60.

The columns of residues are merely arithmetic progressions with common difference a. The numbers directly below an entry n are thus of the form $n + ka$, $k = 1, 2, 3, \ldots$. Consequently, once an attainable number n is encountered in a column, every number $n + ka$ following it in the column is obtainable with k more scores of a points.

Let pb and qb denote any two distinct key multiples of b: i.e., $p \neq q$ and $p, q \in \{0, 1, 2, \ldots, (a - 1)\}$. Now, in order for these multiples to occur in the same column of the table, they must be congruent (mod a):

$$pb \equiv qb \pmod{a}.$$

This gives

$$b(p - q) \equiv 0 \pmod{a}.$$

Since a and b are relatively prime, we obtain $p - q \equiv 0 \pmod{a}$, and

$$p \equiv q \pmod{a}.$$

However, because p and q are different numbers less than a, they lie in different residue classes (mod a). This contradiction establishes that no two of the key multiples of b occur in the same column. Since there are as many key multiples as there are columns in the table, the only alternative is for exactly one multiple to fall in each column.

The next thing to show is that, in every column, the numbers above the key multiple of b are unattainable cumulative scores. If mb denotes a key multiple, then $0 \leqslant m < a$ and a number above it in the same column is given by $mb - ka$ for some natural number k. Supposing such a number is an attainable score, we would have $mb - ka = ax + by$, for some nonnegative integers x and y. This leads to

$$by \leqslant ax + by = mb - ka < mb,$$

that is, $by < mb$, implying $y < m$. Thus m and y are two different numbers less than a. Hence m and y are not congruent (mod a).

On the other hand, two numbers in the same column are congruent (mod a). Consequently, $mb \equiv mb - ka$ (mod a), or $mb \equiv ax + by$ (mod a), giving

$$mb \equiv by \ (\text{mod}\, a), \quad \text{and} \quad m \equiv y \ (\text{mod}\, a),$$

since a and b are relatively prime. Thus we have a contradiction and the numbers in the columns above the key multiples of b are all unattainable scores. Clearly, these are the only unattainable scores.

Since the number of unattainable scores is given in the problem, we may be able to use a general formula for this number. Suppose the key multiple mb occurs in the column headed by the number r. Then $mb = r + ka$ for some nonnegative integer k. In these terms, the multiple mb is the $(k + 1)$-th number in the column, and there are k unattainable numbers above it. Accordingly, the total number of unattainable scores is the sum of the numbers k for all the columns. For each column, we have its key multiple involved in a particular relation

$$mb = r + ka,$$

where m and r are appropriate values in the range $\{0, 1, 2, \ldots, (a - 1)\}$. Over all the columns of the table, each of the values $0, 1, 2, \ldots, (a - 1)$ occurs once and only once as a value of m and also as a value of r. Summing over all the columns, then, we obtain, for m and r,

$$\Sigma m = \Sigma r = 0 + 1 + 2 + \cdots + (a - 1) = \frac{(a - 1)a}{2}.$$

Adding all the equations $mb = r + ka$, we get

$$b \cdot \Sigma m = \Sigma r + a \cdot \Sigma k,$$

$$b \cdot \frac{(a - 1)a}{2} = \frac{(a - 1)a}{2} + a \cdot \Sigma k,$$

$$b \cdot \frac{(a - 1)}{2} = \frac{(a - 1)}{2} + \Sigma k,$$

from which we obtain the desired number of unattainable scores to be

$$\Sigma k = \frac{(a - 1)(b - 1)}{2}.$$

Accordingly, we have $\frac{1}{2}(a - 1)(b - 1) = 35$, or $(a - 1)(b - 1) = 70$. Since a and b are positive integers and $a > b$, the only possible pairs of values for $(a - 1, b - 1)$ are $(70, 1)$, $(35, 2)$, $(14, 5)$, and $(10, 7)$. For the pair (a, b), these yield the values $(71, 2)$, $(36, 3)$, $(15, 6)$, and $(11, 8)$. Because a and b are relatively prime, we eliminate the pairs $(36, 3)$ and $(15, 6)$. If b were to be 2, then 58 would not be an unattainable score. Thus the only values are $a = 11$ and $b = 8$.

We note in passing that the greatest unattainable score occurs in the table just above the greatest key multiple of b, namely $(a - 1)b$. Its value, then, is $(a - 1)b - a$, or $(a - 1)(b - 1) - 1$. Hence the number $(a - 1)(b - 1)$ and all greater numbers are attainable scores.

SOLUTION 2.

A nice derivation of the formula for the number of unattainable scores comes from a consideration of the lattice points (x, y) of a coordinate plane. The solution is then completed as above.

Associated with a cumulative score m are all the pairs of nonnegative integers (x, y) which make $ax + by = m$. That is to say, each attainable score m corresponds to the first quadrant lattice points (x, y) on the line $ax + by = m$ (Figure 115). Clearly each first quadrant lattice point (x, y) on the line $ax + by = m$ provides a way of attaining m as a cumulative score. Since a and b are positive, the slope $-a/b$ of $ax + by = m$ is negative. Consequently, the line $ax + by = m$ intersects the first quadrant in a segment only, the segment joining the points $A(m/a, 0)$ and $B(0, m/b)$. Thus m is an attainable score if and only if the segment AB contains at least one lattice point (x, y). The endpoints A and B, themselves, are acceptable positions for such lattice points.

Now we investigate in general which of the lines $ax + by = m$, m a nonnegative integer, contain lattice points. The Euclidean algorithm provides an integral solution (x, y) to the equation $ax + by = d$, where d denotes the greatest common divisor of a and b. In the case at hand, then, there exists an integral solution to $ax + by = 1$, since a and b are relatively prime. Consequently, for

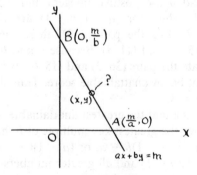

FIG. 115

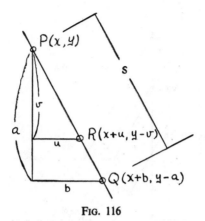

FIG. 116

every $m = 0, 1, 2, \ldots,$ there exists an integral solution making $a(mx) + b(my) = m$. Thus every line in question passes through some lattice point (mx, my). The question is whether or not it is a first-quadrant lattice point.

We observe that if $P(x, y)$ is a lattice point on $ax + by = m$, then the point $Q(x + b, y - a)$ is also a lattice point on the line: we have $a(x + b) + b(y - a) = ax + by = m$. In addition (see Figure 116), we note that no other lattice point $R(x + u, y - v)$ could occur on $ax + by = m$ between P and Q because we would then have the slope $-a/b$ equal to the slope $-v/u$, where v and u are natural numbers which are less, respectively, than a and b, implying that the fraction a/b is not in its lowest terms. This contradicts the fact that a and b are relatively prime. A similar argument shows the same situation on the other ray of $ax + by = m$ which begins at $P(x, y)$. As a result, we see that, for all $m = 0, 1, 2, \ldots,$ the line $ax + by = m$ contains an infinity of lattice points, and that they occur regularly along the line at intervals of $s = \sqrt{a^2 + b^2}$.

The importance of this is that, on any of our lines $ax + by = m$, any interval which is as large as s must contain a lattice point, and that an interval smaller than s can possibly contain at most one lattice point. Consequently, the lines $ax + by = m$ which cross the

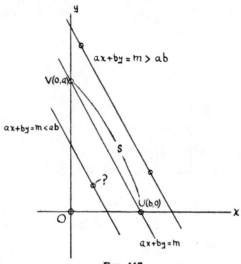

FIG. 117

first quadrant far from the origin have segments of intersection so big that they must contain a lattice point, making the corresponding m an attainable score. However, the lines which cross over close to the origin may or may not pass through a first-quadrant lattice point. Clearly the line $ax + by = m$, whose intersection equals s, separates these classes of lines. The first quadrant intersection of $ax + by = m$ is the segment joining $(m/a, 0)$ and $(0, m/b)$, and has length

$$\sqrt{\frac{m^2}{a^2} + \frac{m^2}{b^2}} = m\sqrt{\frac{1}{a^2} + \frac{1}{b^2}}$$

$$= m\sqrt{\frac{a^2 + b^2}{a^2 b^2}} = \frac{m}{ab} \cdot s.$$

In order for this to equal s, we need $m = ab$. In this case, the intercepts, themselves, are both lattice points, $U(b, 0)$ and $V(0, a)$ (Figure 117). For $m \geqslant ab$, then, we know that $ax + by = m$

passes through a first quadrant lattice point and that m is an attainable score. Incidentally, for $m > ab$, this establishes an important result in Diophantine analysis:

For positive integers a and b, there exists for the equation $ax + by = c$, where $c > ab$, a solution (x, y) in positive integers.

(In this case the segment of intersection exceeds s, implying that a lattice point must occur *internally* in the segment of intersection, thus giving a positive solution.) In any event, our interest here is the conclusion that all the unattainable scores occur among the ab numbers $0, 1, 2, \ldots, (ab - 1)$. We obtain the number of unattainable scores by subtracting from ab the number of attainable ones among $0, 1, 2, \ldots, (ab - 1)$. Our final task, then, is to determine how many attainable scores occur in this range.

We have observed that the intercepts U and V of the critical line $ax + by = ab$ are lattice points whose distance apart along the line is s. Thus no lattice point occurs on this line between U and V. Now, all the lines $ax + by = m$, where $m = 0, 1, 2, \ldots, (ab - 1)$, cut across the first quadrant through the triangle OUV. They constitute a set of equally spaced parallel lines (Figure 118). Each one of the $ax + by = m$ that passes through a lattice point in the triangle OUV denotes an attainable score m, and the lines of the set which thus fail to pick up a lattice point represent unattainable scores. It could be that some of the lattice points of $\triangle OUV$ are picked up and that others are missed. However, we shall show shortly that all of the triangle's lattice points lie on lines of our set. Because the segments of intersection are $< s$, no line can pick up more than one of these lattice points. As a result, the number of attainable scores is just the number of lattice points in $\triangle OUV$. Since the vertices U and V, themselves, correspond to $ax + by = ab$, and we have $m < ab$ for our set of lines, they are not to be counted among the lattice points of $\triangle OUV$. However, since $m = 0$ is under investigation ($m = 0, 1, 2, \ldots, (ab - 1)$), we do count the origin as a lattice point of the triangle. Clearly, the line $ax + by = 0$ picks up the origin, showing 0 to be an attainable score. Let us now prove that every

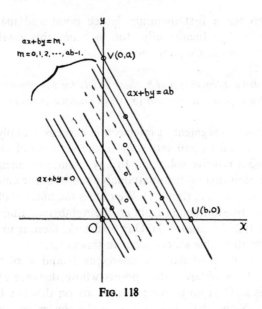

$$ax + by = m,$$
$$m = 0, 1, 2, \cdots, ab-1.$$

$V(0,a)$

$ax + by = ab$

$ax + by = 0$

$U(b,0)$

FIG. 118

other lattice point (x', y') of the $\triangle OUV$ occurs on some line of our set.

We consider the line through (x', y') in the direction of the lines of our set and we show that it is indeed a member of the set. Every line with slope $-a/b$ has equation $ax + by = k$, the particular line through (x', y') having $k = ax' + by'$ (Figure 119). Because a, b, x', and y' are all nonnegative integers, k is also a nonnegative integer. The x-intercept of this line is k/a, and because (x', y') belongs to the triangle OUV, and the line is not the side UV, itself, this x-intercept must be a real number less than the side OU, which has length b. Thus

$$0 \leqslant k/a < b, \quad \text{giving } 0 \leqslant k < ab.$$

Being an integer, k must be one of the numbers $0, 1, 2, \ldots,$

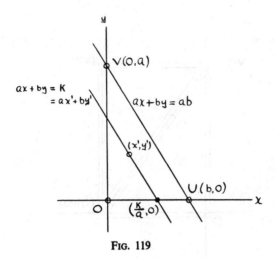

Fig. 119

$(ab - 1)$, making $ax + by = k$ one of the lines $ax + by = m$ of our set.

We conclude by counting the number of lattice points t in the triangle OUV, omitting U and V themselves.

In the closed rectangle with vertices $(0, 0)$, $(b, 0)$, (b, a), $(0, a)$, obtained by reflecting $\triangle OUV$ in the midpoint of UV (Figure 120), we have $2t + 2$ lattice points, counting U and V. The dimensions of this rectangle are a and b, implying that it contains $(a + 1) \cdot (b + 1)$ lattice points. Thus we have $2t + 2 = (a + 1)(b + 1)$, yielding

$$t = \tfrac{1}{2}(a + 1)(b + 1) - 1.$$

This gives the number of attainable scores in the range under investigation, implying that the number of unattainable scores is

$$ab - t = ab - \tfrac{1}{2}(a + 1)(b + 1) + 1$$

$$= \tfrac{1}{2}(a - 1)(b - 1).$$

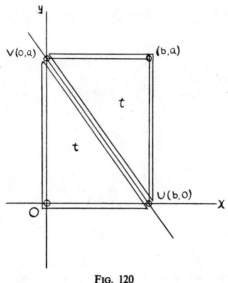

Fig. 120

Exercise

1. Nine lattice points in 3-space are chosen at random (i.e., points (x, y, z) where x, y, z are integers). Prove that at least one of the segments joining these points in pairs passes through a lattice point.

Reference

1. J. H. McKay, The William Lowell Putnam Mathematical Competition, Amer. Math. Monthly, 79 (1973) 170–179, in particular Problem A-5, 174–175.

CHAPTER 14

LOVÁSZ' PROOF OF A THEOREM
OF TUTTE

In recent years the Theory of Graphs has enriched mathematics with a stream of interesting results, techniques, and problems. In May, 1973, the brilliant young Hungarian mathematician László Lovász produced a new proof of an advanced theorem of W. T. Tutte. With a masterly touch, Lovász derived Tutte's deep result with a simple and beautiful line of reasoning.

1. Introduction. In order to understand Lovász' proof, there is no need to review all the fine points of a rigorous development of the subject. However, the background needs to be set. By a graph we mean a finite collection of undefined objects called vertices and a set of edges, each of which relates, that is, joins, a pair of different vertices. For our purposes, nothing is lost by thinking of graphs in terms of their geometric representations, which takes vertices to be points and edges to be arcs of curves. Different configurations which represent the same graph are equivalent. Our deductions must deal with the nature of the underlying graph, not iust with fickle representations. In Graph Theory it is generally immaterial how the vertices are arranged and whether the edges are pictured as straight or curved, as intersecting or not. We note that intersections of edges are not considered as extra vertices of a graph.

There are many kinds of graphs. The subject of Tutte's theorem is the characterization of the graphs which possess a so-called "1-factor." Suppose a graph G has n vertices. A 1-factor of G is simply a set of $n/2$ separate edges which collectively contain all n

of the vertices of G among their endpoints. By "separate" we intend no two of the edges to have a vertex in common. A 1-factor is also called a "matching." (See Figure 121.) Several observations are immediate:

1. If G possesses a 1-factor, then
   (i) G must have an even number of vertices,
   (ii) G can have no isolated vertex (a vertex incident with no edge).
2. If G is a complete graph (i.e., every pair of vertices is joined by an edge) with an even number of vertices, then G has a 1-factor.
3. If G is a complete graph with an odd number of vertices, all but one vertex can be paired up, using separate edges.

The separate pieces of a graph are called its "components." For two vertices to be in the same component, there must be some sequence of edges constituting a path between them. However, there can be no path between vertices of different components. A component is said to be odd or even according to the number of vertices it possesses.

It comes as no surprise that the deletion of a subset S of the vertices of a graph and of the edges incident with these vertices causes a graph to fall apart. This method of reducing a graph plays a major role in what follows. Of course, the deletion of various subsets S brings about various results in a graph. The graph obtained from G by deleting the subset S (and its edges) is denoted $G - S$ (Figure 122).

In a given graph G, suppose that some subset S of vertices has been selected and $G - S$ determined. The number of odd components in $G - S$ is denoted S'. Now in a 1-factor of G all the vertices are matched up. Let us consider the possible matchings of the vertices which belong to the part $G - S$ (Figure 123). It may be possible for the vertices of an even component to be paired up with a set of separate edges which come entirely from their own component. However, in an odd component, at least one vertex is forced to be matched with a vertex outside the component. Consequently, in a 1-factor of G, there are at least S' vertices of

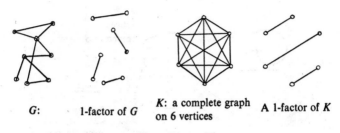

G: 1-factor of G   K: a complete graph   A 1-factor of K
                               on 6 vertices

FIG. 121

$G - S$ (at least one for each odd component in $G - S$) which require matching outside their components. Since there are no edges from one component to another, the only possible source of vertices to meet these demands is S itself. And no two of the unmatched vertices of $G - S$ can be paired off with the same vertex of S because the edges of a 1-factor must be separate. Thus, if G is to possess a 1-factor, S must contain at least S' different vertices and also possess a set of edges capable of accommodating the required matchings. Disregarding this important requirement of a suitable set of edges, we obtain a weak necessary condition for G to have a 1-factor ($|S|$ denotes the number of vertices in the subset S):

for every subset of vertices S, $|S| \geqslant S'$.

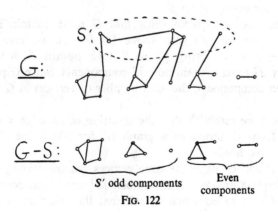

S' odd components   Even
                           components
FIG. 122

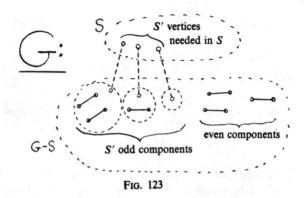

FIG. 123

We note that it is necessary for this condition to hold even for the null set $\varnothing$. For $S = \varnothing$, we have $|S| = 0$, and $G - S = G - \varnothing = G$, itself. Now a graph with a 1-factor cannot have any odd components, for an odd component has to have a vertex which goes unmatched. Thus $S' = 0$, and $|S| \geqslant S'$ holds.

It was Tutte's splendid accomplishment, in 1946, to show that this evidently weak necessary condition is actually a necessary and sufficient condition for a graph G to have a 1-factor. (The factorization of linear graphs, J. London Math. Soc., vol. 22 (1947) 107–111).

2. Preliminaries.

Our goal is to prove that G has a 1-factor if $|S| \geqslant S'$ for every subset S.

(a) The first step is to show that G must contain an even number of vertices. As seen above for $S = \varnothing$, we have $|S| = 0$ and $G - S = G$. Using $|S| \geqslant S'$, we obtain $S' = 0$. Consequently, G must contain no odd components. Since G possesses only even components, the total number of vertices in G must be even.

(b) Next we establish that the insertion of an edge x which is missing from G produces a graph G' for which the condition $|S| \geqslant S'$ also holds.

Since G and G' have the same vertices, we are dealing with the same subsets S and the same numbers $|S|$ when considering G'. It is not difficult to convince oneself that the insertion of an edge cannot increase the number of odd components in a graph. For example, if x joins two odd components of $G - S$, an even component is formed and the value of S' goes down by 2. In all other cases, S' remains unchanged, e.g., if x is incident with S, then it is deleted with S and $G' - S$ is identical to $G - S$. Since $|S| \geqslant S'$ is valid for G, it holds also for G'.

(c) The persistence of the property $|S| \geqslant S'$ throughout the addition of a missing edge, and therefore throughout the addition of any number of missing edges, leads to one of the key ideas in the proof.

Suppose a graph G, which has an even number of vertices, does not possess a 1-factor. The insertion of missing edges might well change a graph into one which does have a 1-factor. Wishing to avoid the creation of a 1-factor, let us insert only those edges which do not complete a 1-factor in the resulting graph. Let each missing edge be tested: those edges which do not complete a 1-factor are left in the graph, while edges which do complete a 1-factor are taken back out. After testing all the missing edges, one obtains a graph G^* which still has no 1-factor but which is "saturated" in the sense that the insertion now of any missing edge would necessarily complete a 1-factor (otherwise the edge would not now be missing). Since the number of vertices is even, G^* cannot be a complete graph (for then it would have a 1-factor). It is incomplete but saturated. In general, various saturated graphs may be obtained from a given graph by testing the missing edges in different orders. For each of them, the condition $|S| \geqslant S'$ holds. Lovász cleverly exploits this notion of a saturated graph.

3. Lovász' Proof.

Lovász proceeds indirectly. Suppose G, while satisfying $|S| \geqslant S'$ for all subsets S, does not possess a 1-factor. He deduces a contradiction.

We have seen that G must have an even number of vertices. Since G has no 1-factor, then G cannot be a complete graph. Inserting the appropriate edges, then, we can embed G in a saturated graph G^* which also has no 1-factor and is not complete. It is immaterial which of the possible saturated graphs one obtains. It is the fact that G^* has no 1-factor which will eventually

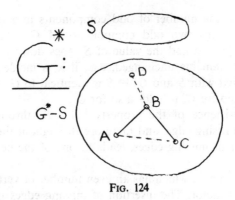

give us our final contradiction. From now on we consider the graph G^*.

Let S denote the subset of vertices of G^*, possibly an empty set, each of which is joined to *every* other vertex in G^*. Singling out this particular subset S for special consideration is unlikely enough. At this point, however, Lovász' piercing insight laid hold of the possibility that every component of $G^* - S$ is, itself, a complete graph, and his marvellous ingenuity enabled him to prove it. The theorem follows quickly on the heels of this masterstroke. We proceed with the lemma:

(a) *If A, B, C are vertices of $G^* - S$ and the edges AB and BC occur in $G^* - S$, then the edge AC also must occur in $G^* - S$.*

This is the main thrust of the whole proof. Our attack is again indirect. Suppose that the edge AC does not occur in $G^* - S$. (See Figure 124.)

Since G^* is saturated, it is generally more useful to know that an edge is missing than to know that it occurs in the graph. Accordingly, the insertion of the edge AC in the saturated G^* would give us a graph $G^* \cup AC$ which must have a 1-factor. If more than one 1-factor results, pick any one of them and call it M. If M does not employ the edge AC, itself, then G^* would already possess the 1-factor M without the edge AC, which is not the case. Thus AC is one of the edges used in M.

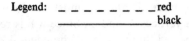

Legend: _ _ _ _ _ _ _ _ red
                              black

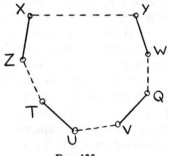

FIG. 125

Because the vertex B occurs in $G^* - S$, it is not one of the special vertices of S which are joined to all other vertices. Consequently, there must be some vertex D to which B is not joined by an edge. This vertex D must also occur in $G^* - S$ since, not being joined to B, it is not a vertex of S. Inserting the edge BD in the saturated G^* gives a graph $G^* \cup BD$ which possesses a 1-factor N (if more than one, choose a definite one for N). And N would have BD as one of its edges. Since the edge BD is not even present in the graph $G^* \cup AC$, BD is not an edge of the 1-factor M. Similarly, AC is not an edge of N. Thus M and N are not identical, although they may have some edges in common.

Let the edges of M be colored red and those of N be colored black. Now delete the edges which are common to M and N. At least the red edge AC and the black one BD must remain. We deduce easily that there are other edges of M and N which are not deleted. Suppose XY denotes a red edge which survives the deletions (at least AC is available to play the role of XY). Since XY is not deleted as an edge common to M and N, it cannot also be a black edge of N (see Figure 125). However, the edges of the 1-factor N do pair up all the vertices of the graph G^*. Thus X must be an endpoint of some black edge XZ in N. Similarly, there must be a black edge YW in N. Since XY is not black and the edges of N are separate, Z and W must be distinct from each other and from the vertices X and Y. Since XY is red, neither XZ nor YW can also be red, implying that the edges XZ and YW are not common to M and N, and are thus not deleted.

The same kind of argument leads to red edges ZT and WQ which are not deleted. However, it is possible this time for T to be the vertex W and Q the vertex Z, making both these red edges the same edge ZW. This would close a cycle $ZXYW$ of alternating red and black edges. Otherwise, an extended arc $TZXYWQ$ results. By similar arguments, we can always deduce, from the existence of such an unclosed arc, either a further two-way extension of the arc or the completion of a cycle with alternating colors. Since the edges of a 1-factor are separate, it is impossible for the extensions of an arc to double back onto a vertex of the arc itself (except when closing a cycle, which merely connects the open ends of the arc). Because G^* contains a finite number of vertices, extensions of an arc cannot go on forever. That is to say, at some point the arc must close into a cycle of alternating red and black edges. Of course, over the entire extent of G^* many such cycles might occur.

The fact that the undeleted edges of M and N go together in such cycles is of vital importance to the proof. We now turn our attention to the particular cycle K in which the remaining red edge AC occurs. There are two cases: the edge BD, which also remains, may or may not also belong to this cycle K.

(i) *If BD does not belong to K*:   The edge BD is the only edge needed in G^* to complete the black 1-factor N (see Figure 126). Since BD does not belong to K, the black edges which do occur there must be edges of G^*. Similarly, AC completes the red 1-factor M. Since AC does belong to K, we may conclude that the red edges of M which occur in $G^* - K$ (i.e., which do not belong to K) are also edges of G^*.

Now in M, the red edges of $G^* - K$ take care of matching up all the vertices in $G^* - K$. And as far as K itself goes, the alternating black edges equally well accomplish the pairing. Thus M's red edges in $G^* - K$, combined with the black edges of K, constitute a complete 1-factor of G^*. Since all these edges do belong to G^*, G^* has a 1-factor, a contradiction.

Legend: ─ ─ ─ ─ ─ ─ ─ ─ red
         ────────────── black
         ++++++++++++++++++ AB, BC

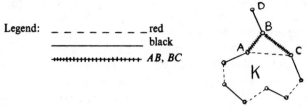

FIG. 126

(ii) *If BD does occur in K*: Neither *AB* nor *BC* can be a red
edge of *M* (because *AC* is), or a black edge of *N* (because *BD* is);
see Figure 127. Consequently, neither *AB* nor *BC* is an edge of *K*.
The cyclic order of the points around *K* is either *ADBC* or *ABDC*.
These lead to equivalent cases. For definiteness, suppose the order
is *ADBC*. Let K_1 denote the arc of *K* between *B* and *C* which does
not contain *D*.

Now the edges of *K* alternate in color. Because *BD* is black and
AC red, the arc K_1 must begin at *B* with a red edge and end at *C*
with a black one. Adding the edges *AB* and *AC* to K_1 then
completes a cycle *L* in which the edges alternate in color with the
exception of *AB*. In particular, his cycle does not contain the edge
BD. (Whatever be the case of the cyclic order of *A*, *D*, *B*, and *C*
around *K*, the edge *AB* or the edge *BC*, coupled with *AC*, can be
used to complete a cycle like *L* which contains *A*, *B*, and *C* but

Legend: ─ ─ ─ ─ ─ ─ ─ ─ red
         ────────────── black
         ++++++++++++++++++ AB, BC

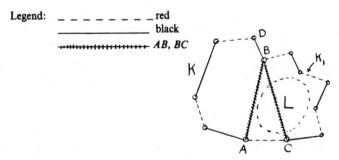

FIG. 127

avoids D.) Consequently, the black edges of L all belong to G^*. Since L does contain AC, all the red edges not in L (i.e., in $G^* - L$) are also edges of G^*.

In M, the red edges of L pair up the vertices of L, and the rest of them match the vertices of $G^* - L$. However, the vertices of L can equally well be paired up by using the black edges of L supplemented by the edge AB. Thus the set of edges consisting of the edge AB, the black edges of L, and the red edges not in L, all of which belong to G^*, constitute a 1-factor of G^*. This second contradiction completes the indirect proof of our fundamental lemma.

(b) *The Components of $G^* - S$ are Complete.*

It is easy now to deduce that the components of $G^* - S$ are complete, that is, in each component every pair of vertices is joined by an edge. Let A and B denote two vertices in the same component of $G^* - S$ (Figure 128). Then there exists in the component some sequence of edges constituting a path $AXYZ \ldots TB$ between them. By the result we have just proved, it follows that there must be an edge joining A to each vertex in the path. Since AX and XY join vertices in $G^* - S$, we have, by the lemma, that AY must also occur in $G^* - S$; similarly, AY and YZ lead to the edge AZ, etc., all the way to the edge AB, itself.

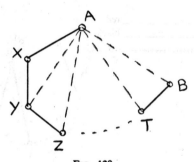

FIG. 128

(c) *The Final Contradiction.*

Because the components of $G^* - S$ are complete, the vertices of $G^* - S$ can almost be paired up with separate edges inside $G^* - S$ itself. The vertices of an even component can be done completely, and only one vertex of an odd component need go unmatched. Because $|S| \geqslant S'$, S contains enough vertices so that a different vertex of S may be assigned to each odd component of $G^* - S$ (Figure 129). Since each vertex of S is joined to every other vertex in the entire graph G^*, there exist edges from these assigned vertices of S to the unmatched vertices in the odd components of $G^* - S$, effecting a matching for all these outstanding vertices of $G^* - S$.

This leaves unmatched only other vertices in S itself, if there are any. The number of such vertices remaining in S must be even, because an even number of vertices have been matched so far (they have been done in pairs) and the total number of vertices in G^* is even. And, being in S, each such vertex is joined to each of the others. Thus there is no difficulty in pairing them up with their own edges to complete an entire 1-factor in G^*. With this contradiction the proof is complete.

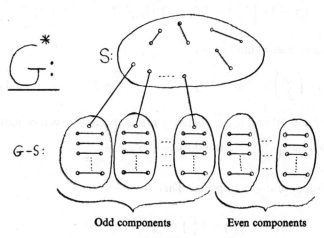

Odd components   Even components

FIG. 129

SOLUTIONS TO THE EXERCISES

1. Three Surprises from Combinatorics and Number Theory.

1.

$$\binom{2p}{p} = \frac{(2p)!}{p!p!} = \frac{2p(2p-1)(2p-2)\cdots(2p-p+1)}{p!}$$

$$= \frac{2(2p-1)\cdot\;\cdot(p+1)}{(p-1)!}.$$

Thus

$$(p-1)!\binom{2p}{p} = 2(2p-1)(2p-2)\cdots(p+1).$$

Since $p + r \equiv r \pmod{p}$, we have

$$(p-1)!\binom{2p}{p} \equiv 2(p-1)(p-2)\cdots(1) = 2[(p-1)!]\pmod{p}.$$

Since $(p-1)!$ and p are relatively prime (because p is a prime), it follows that $\binom{2p}{p} \equiv 2 \pmod{p}$.

2. Suppose $n = p$, a prime. Then

$$\binom{n}{r} = \binom{p}{r} = \frac{p!}{r!(p-r)!},$$

yielding

$$r!\binom{p}{r} = p(p-1)\cdots(p-r+1).$$

Since $1 \leqslant r \leqslant p-1$, the prime factor p does not occur in $r!$. But, since p divides the right-hand side, it must also divide the left-hand side. Accordingly, p divides $\binom{p}{r}$, i.e., n divides $\binom{n}{r}$.

Conversely, suppose n divides $\binom{n}{r}$ for $r = 1, 2, \ldots, n-1$. Then we have

$$M = \frac{1}{n}\binom{n}{r} = \frac{(n-1)(n-2)\cdots(n-r+1)}{r!}$$

is an integer. Let p denote a prime divisor of n. If $n \neq p$, then $p < n$, placing p among the numbers $(1, 2, \ldots, n-1)$, the range of r. Consider the case $r = p$. The denominator of M, $p!$, contains the prime factor p. However none of the factors in the numerator is divisible by p:

$$p \nmid n - i \quad \text{for } i = 1, 2, \ldots, p-1.$$

Hence, for $r = p$, M does not reduce to an integer, giving a contradiction. Thus $n = p$.

2. Four Minor Gems from Geometry.

1. On BA lay off $BM = p/2$ (Figure 130). Draw the circle K which touches AB at M and also touches BC. Then K touches BC at N, where $BN = BM$. Then the tangent from X to K which is closer to B determines a $\triangle PQB$ with perimeter p. If the tangent touches K at L, then $PL = PM$ and $QL = QN$. Thus the perimeter of $\triangle PQB$ is $BP + PL + LQ + QB = BM + BN = 2BM = p$.

2. Let circle K (Figure 131) touch AB and AC and pass through X (the construction of this circle is a particular case of the famous

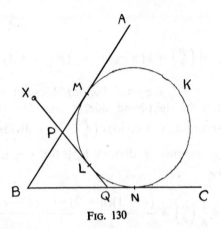

FIG. 130

Problem of Apollonius). There are two circles satisfying this condi-tion. Let K denote the larger one. Then the tangent to K at X gives the required $\triangle PQB$.

As in Exercise 1, the perimeter of $\triangle PQB$ is $2BM$. Since PXQ is a tangent, any other line ST through X is a secant of K. However, the perimeter of $\triangle STB$ is twice the distance from B to the point of contact M' of a circle K' which touches AB, AC and ST (see Exercise 1). Because ST is a secant of K, the circle K' must be a larger circle than K, implying BM' exceeds BM. Thus $\triangle PQB$ has minimal perimeter.

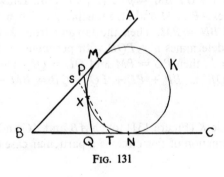

FIG. 131

3. Let the quadrilateral be $ABCD$ (Figure 132) with points of contact P, Q, R, S. Let the length of the tangents from A, B, C, D, respectively, be a, b, c, d. At A, B, C, D suspend, respectively, masses of $1/a, 1/b, 1/c, 1/d$. Then the center of gravity of the masses at adjacent vertices is the point of contact of the side they determine. Thus the masses $1/a$ and $1/b$ have center of gravity at P, and $1/c, 1/d$ at R. Consequently, the center of gravity G of the entire system must occur on PR. But, similarly, G must lie on QS. Thus PR and QS must intersect at G. Because they intersect, they determine a plane π. The plane π intersects the sphere in a circle which contains the four points of contact P, Q, R, S.

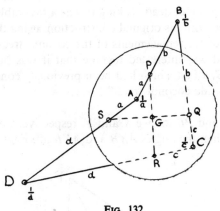

FIG. 132

4. Clearly the triangle AC_1B_1 (Figure 133) is congruent to the triangle A_1C_1B (SAS). Also a quarter turn about C_1 carries the one into coincidence with the other. Thus AB_1 and A_1B are perpendicular. That is, AB subtends a right angle at P_1. Similarly, AB subtends a right angle at P_2 and P_3, implying that the circumcircle of $\triangle P_1P_2P_3$ is just the circle on AB as diameter. The treasure is therefore buried at the midpoint of AB.

The following solution was given in the American Mathematical

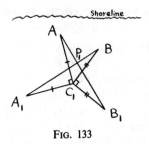

FIG. 133

Monthly, (65) (1958), p. 448, by R. R. Seeber, Jr., IBM Corp. Poughkeepsie, New York:

"While wondering how to proceed, the pirate watched three sea gulls engaged in a violent aerial battle. Presently all three birds fluttered to the ground, dead. Taking this as a favorable omen, the pirate proceeded with his original construction, using the locations of the three birds for replacements of the coconut trees. He found his treasure and was interested to note that it was buried at the midpoint of AB, a fact which had been previously concealed by a clump of shore-side coconut trees."

5. Draw PA and PB to give X and Y, respectively, on the circle (Figure 134). Then the angles AXB and AYB are right angles. For

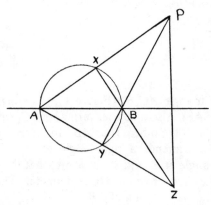

FIG. 134

$\triangle ABP$, then, AY and BX are two altitudes. Their point of intersection Z, then, is the orthocenter, and PZ is the required third altitude.

4. The Generation of Prime Numbers.

1. Suppose, if possible, that an integer d between 1 and 41 divides a value of $f(x) = x^2 + x + 41$. Divide the value of x in question by d to yield $x = kd + r$, where the remainder r is subject to $0 \leqslant r < d$. Then

$$f(x) = f(kd + r) = (kd + r)^2 + (kd + r) + 41$$

$$= d(k^2d + 2rk + k) + r^2 + r + 41$$

$$= d(k^2d + 2rk + k) + f(r).$$

Since d divides $f(x)$, d also divides $f(r)$. However, this is impossible. The number r is among $0, 1, \ldots, d - 1$, where $d - 1 \leqslant 39$, and therefore $f(r)$ is one of the numbers $f(0), f(1), \ldots, f(39)$. But these values of $f(x)$ are known to be the primes 41, 43, 47, ..., 1601, each of which exceeds d. Thus d cannot divide $f(r)$.

2. For $x = -40, -39, \ldots, 39$, we know that $f(x)$ is a prime, and therefore not a square. For $x = -41$ and $x = 40$, $f(x)$ is clearly a square.

Consider $x > 40$. For $x = 41$, we have $f(41) = 41 \cdot 43$, which is not a square. For $x = 42, 43, 44, \ldots$, we have $f(x) = x^2 + x + 41 > x^2$, while $f(x - 1) = x^2 - x + 41 < x^2$,

$$\text{i.e., } f(x - 1) < x^2 < f(x).$$

Thus the squares, x^2, occur between consecutive values of $f(x)$ without ever coinciding with any of them. The range $x < -41$ is handled similarly.

3. Let $f(0) \cdot f(1) \cdot f(2) \cdots f(39) = K$. Then $f(K + r)$ is com-

posite for $r = 0, 1, 2, \ldots, 39$. We have

$$f(K + r) = (K + r)^2 + (K + r) + 41 = K(K + 2r + 1) + f(r),$$

which is clearly divisible by $f(r)$, a nontrivial factor.

4. The least prime is 2, implying that p is at least 12. If none of p_1, p_2, p_3, is 3, then each is congruent (mod 3) to ± 1. Thus

$$p \equiv p_1^2 + p_2^2 + p_3^2 \equiv 1 + 1 + 1 \equiv 0 \;(\text{mod } 3),$$

contradicting the primality of p since p is at least 12. Thus at least one of p_1, p_2, p_3, is 3.

5. For $p = 2$, $2^p + 3^p = 13$, which is not a power. For $p = 5$, $2^p + 3^p = 275$, which is not a power. Otherwise, for p an odd prime $2k + 1$, we have

$$2^p + 3^p = 2^{2k+1} + 3^{2k+1}$$

$$= (2 + 3)(2^{2k} - 2^{2k-1} \cdot 3 + 2^{2k-2} \cdot 3^2 - \cdots + 3^{2k})$$

$$= 5(2^{2k} - 2^{2k-1} \cdot 3 + \cdots + 3^{2k}).$$

This implies 5 divides $2^p + 3^p$. We show now that 5^2 does not divide it, implying that it is not a power. We show that 5 does not divide the second term.

Modulo 5, we have $3 \equiv -2$, giving

$$2^{2k} - 2^{2k-1} \cdot 3 + 2^{2k-2} \cdot 3^2 - \cdots + 3^{2k}$$

$$\equiv 2^{2k} - 2^{2k-1}(-2) + 2^{2k-2}(-2)^2 - \cdots + (-2)^{2k}$$

$$= 2^{2k} + 2^{2k} + 2^{2k} + \cdots + 2^{2k}$$

$$= (2k + 1)2^{2k} = p \cdot 2^{p-1}.$$

Now $p \neq 5$, implying 5 does not divide p. Also 5 does not divide 2^{p-1}. The conclusion follows.

5. Two Combinatorial Proofs.

1. Adjacent to each acute angle there occurs an obtuse exterior angle. Since the sum of all the exterior angles is $360°$ for every n-gon, there could not be more than 3 which are obtuse. This means that there are not more than 3 interior angles which are acute. Since many triangles actually achieve this number, it is indeed the maximum.

2. The given prime p is relatively prime to 10. Thus, by Fermat's theorem, we have $p | 10^{p-1} - 1 = 99 \ldots 9 = 9(11 \ldots 1)$, containing $p - 1$ 1's. Since p is also relatively prime to 3, p must divide the factor $11 \ldots 1$.

3. Let V_i and F_i denote the number of vertices and faces, respectively, which are incident with i edges. Then

$$V = V_3 + V_4 + \cdots, \quad F = F_3 + F_4 + \cdots.$$

Counting the endpoints, we have $3V_3 + 4V_4 + \cdots = 2E$, since each edge has two endpoints. Also, counting the edges around the faces, we get $3F_3 + 4F_4 + \cdots = 2E$, because each edge bounds two faces. By Euler's formula, we have $V - E + F = 2$, or $4V - 4E + 4F = 8$, giving

$$4(V_3 + V_4 + \cdots) - (3V_3 + 4V_4 + 5V_5 + \cdots)$$
$$- (3F_3 + 4F_4 + 5F_5 + \cdots) + 4(F_3 + F_4 + \cdots) = 8$$
$$V_3 + F_3 = 8 + (V_5 + 2V_6 + 3V_7 + \cdots)$$
$$+ (F_5 + 2F_6 + 3F_7 + \cdots) \geqslant 8.$$

If $V_3 = 0$, then $F_3 \geqslant 8$, implying at least 8 triangular faces.

4. The number of permutations of n different things taken r at a

time is $n(n - 1) \cdots (n - r + 1) = n!/r!$. The required total is

$$N = \sum_{r=0}^{r=n} \frac{n!}{r!} = \frac{n!}{0!} + \frac{n!}{1!} + \cdots + \frac{n!}{n!}$$

$$= \frac{n!}{0!} + \frac{n!}{1!} + \cdots + \frac{n!}{n!} + \frac{n!}{(n+1)!} + \frac{n!}{(n+2)!} + \cdots$$

$$- \left[\frac{n!}{(n+1)!} + \frac{n!}{(n+2)!} + \cdots \right]$$

$$= n!e - \left[\frac{1}{n+1} + \frac{1}{(n+1)(n+2)} + \cdots \right].$$

Now

$$\frac{1}{n+1} + \frac{1}{(n+1)(n+2)} + \cdots$$

$$< \frac{1}{n+1} + \frac{1}{(n+1)^2} + \frac{1}{(n+1)^3} + \cdots$$

$$= \frac{\dfrac{1}{n+1}}{1 - \dfrac{1}{n+1}} = \frac{1}{n} \leqslant 1.$$

Thus $N = n!e - k$, where $0 < k < 1$. But N is an integer. Observing that $n!e$ is, itself, not an integer (lest e be rational), we see, because $0 < k < 1$, that $n!e - k$ must be the greatest integer not exceeding $n!e$. Hence $N = [n!e]$, as required.

5. Whatever three vertices are chosen, let the figure be spun until one vertex takes up a fixed position A on the circle. The other two chosen vertices, B and C, then, occur randomly among the other $2n$ possible vertices. The diameter through A splits these n on each side. In order for $\triangle ABC$ to contain the center O, the

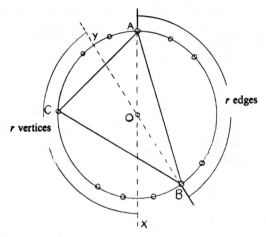

FIG. 135

diameter AX must split B and C. Let the vertex on the "right" side of AX (see Figure 135) be B. Suppose side AB cuts off r edges of the $(2n + 1)$-gon. Let BY denote the diameter through B. Then C must lie in the arc between X and Y, opposite to AB, in order to put O in $\triangle ABC$. Because $2n + 1$ is odd, there is a vertex diametrically opposite each edge of the polygon. Thus, opposite the r edges cut off by AB there are r vertices in the arc XY.

Now the probability of having AB cut off r edges is $1/n$ (because each of the n possible numbers of edges, $1, 2, \ldots, n$, in the "right-hand" semicircle, is equally likely). When we have chosen B, the probability of choosing C so that $\triangle ABC$ contains O is $r/2n - 1$, because there are only $2n - 1$ vertices remaining at this time. Thus the required probability is the sum

$$\sum_{r=1}^{n} \frac{1}{n} \cdot \frac{r}{2n - 1} = \frac{1}{n} \cdot \frac{n(n + 1)}{2(2n - 1)} = \frac{n + 1}{4n - 2}.$$

From the relation that this probability

$$= \frac{\text{the number of triangles containing } O}{\text{the total number of triangles}},$$

we see that the number of triangles which contain the center is

$$\frac{n+1}{4n-2} \cdot \binom{2n+1}{3} = \frac{n+1}{4n-2} \cdot \frac{(2n+1)(2n)(2n-1)}{6}$$

$$= \frac{n(n+1)(2n+1)}{6},$$

which is the sum of the squares of the first n natural numbers. Thus, in passing from a $(2n-1)$-gon to a $(2n+1)$-gon, the number of triangles which contain the center increases by n^2.

7. A Theorem of Gabriel Lamé.

1. Let $N = 11 \ldots 1$, containing n 1's, denote the required number. Let $33 \ldots 3 = 3K$, where K consists of 100 1's. In order for N to be divisible by 3, the sum of its digits, namely n, must be divisible by 3 (rule of 3). We show that in order for N to be divisible by K, n must be a multiple of 100.

Suppose, to the contrary, that $n = 100q + r$, where $0 < r < 100$. Let $11 \ldots 1$, containing r 1's, be denoted R. Then

$$N = 11 \ldots 1$$

$$= \underbrace{(11 \ldots 1)}_{100} \underbrace{(11 \ldots 1)}_{100} \ldots \underbrace{(11 \ldots 1)}_{q\text{th }100} \underbrace{(11 \ldots 1)}_{r}$$

$$= K \cdot 10^{100(q-1)+r} + K \cdot 10^{100(q-2)+r} + \cdots + K \cdot 10^r + R.$$

Thus $N \equiv R \pmod{K}$. If K divides N, then, because $R < K$, it must be that $R = 0$. This means $r = 0$, a contradiction.

Thus, for $3k$ to divide N, we must have n divisible by both 3 and 100, implying 300 divides n. The smallest n, then, is 300.

2. Suppose the divisors of n, in increasing order, are $d_1 = 1, d_2, \ldots, d_k = n$. Then $n/d_1, n/d_2, \ldots, n/d_k$ is the same set

of divisors, in the reverse order. Thus the product

$$(d_1 d_2 \cdots d_k)\left(\frac{n}{d_1} \cdot \frac{n}{d_2} \cdots \frac{n}{d_k}\right) = (d_1 d_2 \cdots d_k)^2.$$

Therefore, $n^k = (d_1 d_2 \cdots d_k)^2$.

3. (a) Let x, y, z denote a set of numbers satisfying the given conditions. Label them so that $x < y < z$.

Now z divides $x + y$. But $x + y < 2z$, implying that z cannot go into $x + y$ more often than once. Thus $z = x + y$.

This makes $x + z = 2x + y$, and this is divisible by y. Consequently, y must divide $2x$. However, $2x < 2y$, implying that y could not go into $2x$ more than once. Thus $y = 2x$. This makes $z = x + y = 3x$.

Consequently, the numbers are $x, 2x, 3x$. Since they are coprime in pairs, then x must be 1. Hence the set $(1, 2, 3)$ is the unique solution to the problem.

(b) Let $a < b < c$ denote a set of numbers which satisfy the given conditions. Then $ab/c = x + (1/c)$, or $ab - 1 = cx$ for some positive integral quotient x. We have

$$cx = ab - 1 < ab < ac, \quad \text{implying that } x < a.$$

This means that $x < b$, too.

We have also $ac/b = y + (1/b)$, giving $ac - 1 = by$. Thus b divides $ac - 1$, and $x(ac - 1)$ as well. Now

$$x(ac - 1) = acx - x = a(ab - 1) - x = a^2 b - (a + x).$$

Thus b divides $a + x$.

In a similar way, we see that a divides $b + x$. As in part (a), because $x < a < b$, we have $a + x < 2b$, implying $a + x = b$. Then $b + x = a + 2x$, which is divisible by a. This shows that a divides $2x$. Yet $2x < 2a$, implying that $a = 2x$. In turn, then, $b = 3x$. Then $ab - 1 = cx$ gives

$$6x^2 - 1 = cx, \quad \text{implying that } x \text{ divides } -1.$$

Thus $x = 1$, giving the unique set $(2, 3, 5)$ for (a, b, c).

4. Since $a^3 - b^3 - c^3 = 3abc$, we have $b < a$ and $c < a$. This implies that $b + c < 2a$, and $2(b + c) < 4a$. Consequently,

$$a^2 < 4a, \quad \text{giving } a < 4.$$

However, $a^2 = 2(b + c)$ implies that a^2 is even. Thus a is even, making $a = 2$. As a result, $b + c = 2$, making $b = c = 1$.

5. The conclusion follows the demonstration of any example in which the number of steps in the Euclidean algorithm is actually 5 times the number of digits in the smaller number. Such an example is given by the consecutive Fibonacci numbers 8 and 13, which require $5 \cdot 1$ steps.

8. Box-Packing Problems.

1.

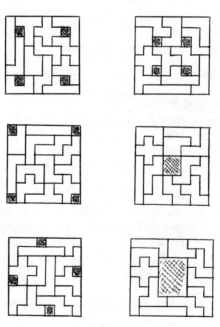

FIG. 136

2. In an ordinary checkerboard coloring, the *F*-hexomino covers 4 squares of one color and 2 of the other. It follows, as for the *L*-tetromino, that this *F* is even ($4x + 2y = 2x + 4y$ giving $x = y$, etc.). Also, any number of these *F*'s placed end to end provides an even polyomino. The polyominoes thus formed by *n* *F*'s, $n = 1, 2, 3, \ldots,$ constitute an infinity of even polyominoes which are clearly dissimilar in shape (Figure 137). Since 15 copies of the *L*-tromino pack a 5×9 rectangle, as shown in Figure 138, the *L*-tromino is odd. From this single specimen we can generate an infinite family of dissimilar odd polyominoes. Simply blow up the packed 5×9 rectangle uniformly until its dimensions are $5a \times 9b$ (i.e., stretch it by a factor of "*a*" in one direction, and by a factor of *b* in the other). This transforms each of the *L*-trominoes into polyominoes *M* with outer edges $2a$ and $2b$, as shown. (Since an *L*-tromino is symmetric, whichever way it is packed in the 5×9 rectangle, it is transformed into a copy of *M*.) However, there are still 15 polyominoes in the packing of the larger rectangle. Thus *M* is odd. By letting *a* and *b* vary over relatively prime pairs of increasing values, an infinite family of dissimilar odd polyominoes is generated. The diagrams in Figure 139 show that the *P*-pentomino and the *L*-pentomino are odd.

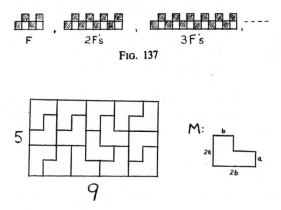

F , 2F's , 3F's , - - - -

FIG. 137

FIG. 138

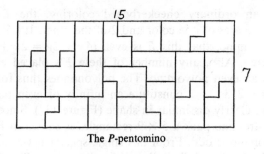

The *P*-pentomino

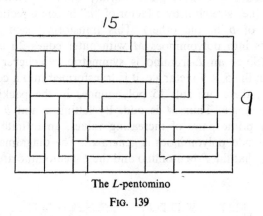

The *L*-pentomino

FIG. 139

3. THEOREM.   *An $a \times b$ rectangle R can be packed with $1 \times n$ rods if and only if n divides a or n divides b.*

Proof. (1) *Sufficiency*:   Clearly, if n divides a, then R can be packed with b columns of a/n rods. Similarly, if n divides b, the conclusion follows (Figure 140).

(2) *Necessity*:   From the existence of a packing of R with $\times n$ rods, we must deduce that n divides either a or b.

First we construct a stained-glass window W by repeating the basic rectangle D (Figure 141), which is an $n \times n$ square, colored with n colors 1 2, 3, . . . , n so that each color occurs exactly once

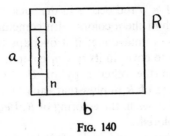

FIG. 140

in each row and each column as shown. Note that the color 1 occurs down the main diagonal. This stained-glass window W is used to induce a coloring of the $a \times b$ rectangle R by placing W on R so that one of the basic units D occurs in the upper left corner of R (Figure 142).

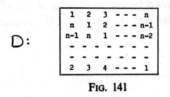

FIG. 141

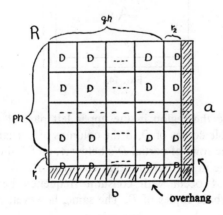

FIG. 142

Now wherever a $1 \times n$ rod occurs in the packing of R, it covers a unit square of each of the n colors—if it coincides with a row or column of a D, this is immediate; if it overlaps two copies of D, then the cells it fails to cover in its row or column are precisely the cells it picks up in the other copy of D. Consequently, the existence of a packing of R implies that each of the colors occurs the same number of times in the coloring of R. Let us say that R is thus "uniformly" colored.

Suppose that neither a nor b is divisible by n, but that

$$a = pn + r_1, \quad \text{and} \quad b = qn + r_2, \quad \text{where } 0 < r_1, r_2 < n.$$

The right-hand edge of R, then, slices down through a column of D's in the window so that the first r_2 columns of the D's cover R while the remaining columns hang over the edge of R. Similarly at the bottom of R we have the top r_1 rows of the D's covering R while the rest hang down below R. Let us shear off the overlapping parts, and consider just the region of the rectangle R (Figure 143).

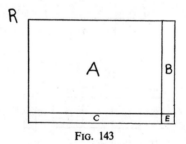

Fig. 143

Let A denote the region in the upper left part of R which is covered by whole copies of D, B the columns of partial D's to the right of A, C the rows of partial D's below A, and E the remaining $r_1 \times r_2$ rectangle in the bottom right corner of R. Now the colors in the region A occur with constant frequency because A is covered with whole copies of D. The same, however, is true of B

and C because they contain, respectively, an integral number of whole columns and rows of D. Since R, too, possesses a uniform coloring, we have, by subtraction, that the rectangle E must also have this property. We shall soon see that this is impossible.

E is an $r_1 \times r_2$ rectangle (Figure 144) which is cut out of the upper left corner of a copy of D. Accordingly, the color 1 occurs in E along a "diagonal" line, as shown. Thus the number of times 1 occurs in E is the smaller of the two dimensions r_1 and r_2 (either one if they are equal). For definiteness, suppose this is r_1. Since every color occurs the same number of times in E, each color must occur r_1 times, implying that the total number of cells in E is nr_1. However, E contains $r_1 r_2$ cells. Thus $r_1 r_2 = nr_1$, giving $r_2 = n$, a contradiction. Thus the theorem is proved.

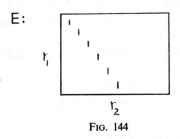

FIG. 144

We observe that a covering of an $a \times b$ rectangle R with $c \times d$ rectangles gives a covering of R by both $c \times 1$ strips (a $c \times d$ rectangle is d strips $c \times 1$) and $1 \times d$ strips (a $c \times d$ rectangle is c strips $1 \times d$). Thus, by Klarner's theorem, c divides a or b, and d divides a or b. The rest is left to the reader.

FIG. 146

4. *Klarner's Own First Solution to His Puzzle.*

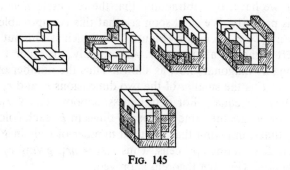

FIG. 145

5. Copies of the composite piece shown (Figure 146), formed by six of the given pieces, will fit together to cover the entire plane.

9. A Theorem of Bang and the Isosceles Tetrahedron.

1. Let AP, AQ meet $\triangle BCD$ at P', Q' and let $P'Q'$ strike the boundary of $\triangle BCD$ at P_1 and Q_1 (Figure 147). Suppose, for definiteness, that P_1 lies on BC. Then, because $ABCD$ is regular, $P_1A = P_1D$. Now, no matter where Q_1 occurs on BD or CD, the length of P_1Q_1 cannot exceed P_1D (the farthest point in an

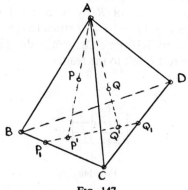

FIG. 147

equilateral triangle from a point on a side is the opposite vertex). Thus

$$P_1A = P_1D \geqslant P_1Q_1.$$

Similarly (supposing Q_1 to be on CD), $Q_1A = Q_1B \geqslant Q_1P_1$. Thus the side P_1Q_1 is minimal in $\triangle P_1Q_1A$. This means that $\angle P_1AQ_1$ is minimal in $\triangle P_1Q_1A$, making it no greater than 60°. Since $\angle PAQ$ is less than $\angle P_1AQ_1$, $\angle PAQ$ must be less than 60°.

10. An Intriguing Series.

1.

$$1 + \frac{1}{3} + \frac{1}{5} + \frac{1}{7} + \frac{1}{9} + \frac{1}{11} + \frac{1}{13} + \cdots$$

$$= \left(1 + \cdots + \frac{1}{9}\right) + \left(\frac{1}{11} + \cdots + \frac{1}{99}\right)$$

$$+ \left(\frac{1}{111} + \cdots + \frac{1}{999}\right) + \cdots \quad **$$

$$< 2 + 25\left(\frac{1}{11}\right) + 125\left(\frac{1}{111}\right) + 625\left(\frac{1}{1111}\right) + \cdots$$

$$< 2 + 25\left(\frac{1}{10}\right) + 125\left(\frac{1}{100}\right) + 625\left(\frac{1}{1000}\right) + \cdots$$

$$= 2 + \frac{25}{10}\left(1 + \frac{5}{10} + \frac{5^2}{10^2} + \cdots\right)$$

$$= 2 + \frac{5}{2}\left[\frac{1}{1 - \frac{1}{2}}\right] = 2 + 5 = 7.$$

**It is not difficult to convince oneself that each large bracket here contains 5 times as many terms as the immediately preceding one. Each denominator in a bracket occurs in the next bracket preceded by each of the 5 digits 1, 3, 5, 7, 9.

2. If

$$S = 1 + \frac{1}{2} + \frac{1}{3} + \frac{1}{4} + \frac{1}{5} + \frac{1}{6} + \cdots,$$

then

$$S > \frac{1}{2} + \frac{1}{2} + \frac{1}{4} + \frac{1}{4} + \frac{1}{6} + \frac{1}{6} + \cdots$$

$$= 1 + \frac{1}{2} + \frac{1}{3} + \cdots$$

$$= S.$$

3. *Solution* 1.

$$e^x = 1 + x + \frac{x^2}{2!} + \cdots > 1 + x.$$

Thus

$$e^N = e^{1 + 1/2 + 1/3 + \cdots + 1/n}$$

$$= e^1 \cdot e^{1/2} \cdot e^{1/3} \cdots e^{1/n}$$

$$> (1 + 1)\left(1 + \frac{1}{2}\right)\left(1 + \frac{1}{3}\right) \cdots \left(1 + \frac{1}{n}\right)$$

$$= 2 \cdot \left(\frac{3}{2}\right) \cdot \left(\frac{5}{3}\right) \cdots \left(\frac{n+1}{n}\right) = n + 1.$$

Solution 2. We observe that the inequality holds for $n = 1$. Now, if

$$e^{1 + 1/2 + 1/3 + \cdots + 1/k} > k + 1,$$

then

$$e^{1 + 1/2 + 1/3 + \cdots + 1/k + 1/(k+1)}$$

$$= (e^{1 + 1/2 + 1/3 + \cdots + 1/k}) \cdot e^{1/(k+1)}$$

$$> (k + 1)\left(1 + \frac{1}{k+1}\right) = k + 2.$$

Thus, by induction, the inequality holds for all n.

Solution 3.

$$N = 1 + \frac{1}{2} + \frac{1}{3} + \cdots + \frac{1}{n} > \int_1^{n+1} \frac{dx}{x} = \ln(n+1).$$

Thus

$$e^N > e^{\ln(n+1)} = n + 1.$$

4. Suppose $1 + 1/2 + 1/3 + \cdots + 1/n = k$, an integer. For some integer r, we have $2^r \leqslant n < 2^{r+1}$. Now every integer may be expressed in the form $m = 2^q t$, where t is odd. Let the denominators be so expressed.

Now

$$n!k = \frac{n!}{1} + \frac{n!}{2} + \cdots + \frac{n!}{2^q t} + \cdots + \frac{n!}{n}.$$

Each term on the right-hand side of this equation reduces to an integer. Since $2^r \leqslant n < 2^{r+1}$, exactly one denominator d contains as many as r factors 2. In the case of this fraction on the right-hand side, the resulting quotient uniquely contains a minimum of (noncancelled) factors 2. Dividing each term of the equation by the number of factors 2 remaining in this "minimal" term, we obtain an even quotient in every case with the single exception of $n!/d$. This term is odd, and, being the only odd term, it makes the right-hand side of the equation an odd number, while the left-hand side remains even. This contradiction establishes the desired result.

12. The Set of Distances Determined by n Points in the Plane.

1. The number n must be at least 3, since, otherwise, the set of points would be collinear. For $n = 3$, a triangle results, and the claim is valid. We proceed by induction. Suppose the claim holds

for n points, and that $A_1, A_2, \ldots, A_{n+1}$ is a set of points, not all collinear. By the known property, some line determined by this set, say $A_n A_{n+1}$, contains only two of the points. Now, either the n points $A_1, A_2, \ldots, A_n$ are collinear or they are not.

Case (i): $A_1, A_2, \ldots, A_n$ are collinear. In this case, A_{n+1} cannot occur on their common line (lest all $n + 1$ points be collinear), implying that $A_{n+1}A_1, A_{n+1}A_2, \ldots, A_{n+1}A_n$ are different lines. With $A_1 A_n$ these yield a total of $n + 1$ different lines.

Case (ii): $A_1, A_2, \ldots, A_n$ are not collinear. In this case, the induction hypothesis guarantees n different lines among these n points $A_1, A_2, \ldots, A_n$. Each of these lines contains at least two of these n points. The line $A_n A_{n+1}$, then, is a new line, for it contains only one of these n points (namely A_n). Thus we again have a total of at least $n + 1$ lines, and the conclusion follows by induction.

13. A Putnam Paper Problem.

1. There are 8 classifications of lattice points (x, y, z) according to the parity of x, y, and z (e.g., x odd, y even, and z odd). Diiichlet's pigeon-hole principle implies that some two of nine lattice points belong to the same class. If they are (x_1, y_1, z_1) and (x_2, y_2, z_2), their midpoint

$$\left(\frac{x_1 + x_2}{2}, \frac{y_1 + y_2}{2}, \frac{z_1 + z_2}{2} \right)$$

is a lattice point, since the numerators in the coordinates are all even (being the sum of two numbers with the same parity).

INDEX